WASHINGTON

JOBS

HOW TO FIND & GET THE JOB YOU <u>WANT</u> IN THE WASHINGTON AREA

BETH CAMPBELL

VANDAMERE PRESS
a division of AB Associates

Published by Vandamere Press
A division of AB Associates
P.O. Box 5243
Arlington, Virginia
22205

Copyright 1992 by Vandamere Press

ISBN 0-918339-21-9

Manufactured in the United States of America. This book is set in
Life by Scott Photographics of Riverdale, Maryland.

Acknowledgements

I would like to thank the many people who helped me produce this resource. My publisher, Art Brown, provided his usual mix of vision, professionalism, and ease. My editor, Pat Berger, imparted her irreplaceable steadfastness and expertise. I also thank others who contributed to the work: Troy Acree, Anne Aitken, Phil Bigler, Bill Boczany, Tom Boone, Stephanie Brown, Carol Covin, Dick Cramer, Charles Daugherty, Debbie Grimes, Connie Henry, Hatim Heymar, George Lufsey, Charles Miller, Janet Cline Patrick, James Peterson, Janet Roy, Jinny Sargent, Rena Sehgal, Bunny Sheppard, Greg Steadman, Joe Stemple, and Rick Treanor. Thanks also to the many I polled about their respective occupations, the clients whom I served, and the coworkers from whom I learned. Finally, I credit my parents for providing me the wisdom to know the importance of doing what I love, and to temper that with earning a living.

Beth Campbell

P.S. I also apologize to women; I used only masculine pronouns to keep the text from being cumbersome. Someday I hope to lobby Webster's for genderless alternatives.

Contents

CHAPTER ONE   **7**
The Plan: The First Job, Mid-Career Adjustments, Management and Corporate, Other Career Changes

CHAPTER TWO   **19**
The Washington Labor Market: Federal Government, Municipal and State Government, Capitol Hill; the industries of Associations, Engineering, High-Tech, Consulting, Hospitality, Construction and Service, Health Care, Education, Journalism, Law Enforcement, Legal, Financial, Sales, and Administrative/Clerical; and additional sections on Independent Consulting and The Hot Careers

CHAPTER THREE   **40**
Finding the Jobs: Classified Ads, Job Fairs, Joblines, Job Postings, Sign Postings, Career Services, Cold Calling, Cold Calling for future openings, Networking, Temporary Work, Volunteering, Self-employment/Small Business

CHAPTER FOUR   **52**
Contacting the Employer: The Résumé, The Cover Letter and Reference Sheet, Sending the Documents, The Application, The SF-171

CHAPTER FIVE   **71**
Interviewing: Preparation, First Impression, First Half, Second Half—Answering Questions, Asking Questions, Closing, Follow-up Options

Appendix A   **86**
Resources: Books, Directories, Software, Publications

Appendix B   **89**
Government joblines: Federal and Municipal

Appendix C   **132**
   Private sector joblines

Appendix D   **173**
   Employer contact sheet

Appendix E   **174**
   Vita worksheet

Glossary   **176**

Index   **178**

Chapter One
THE PLAN

Looking for work is overwhelming. No matter your age, qualifications, locale, or salary requirements, many unknown variables exist between you and that dream job. The key is to conceptualize your job search plan, so that you focus your time effectively on your targeted jobs. There are different strategies for different situations. In later chapters, we will examine the Washington labor market, learn research techniques for finding different types of jobs, write job-specific résumés, and learn how to participate in successful interviews. The first step, however, is formulating your plan. By developing a realistic plan and being adaptable to changes in the labor market, you can guide your career and plan your future.

How hard are you willing to work to find the livelihood you want? Just by reading this book, you are showing you have an active agenda headed in a positive direction. The first step of the plan is to prioritize your reasons for working. The most basic considerations are whether you need a job immediately, or whether you want to improve your career and have the means to pick and choose.

Some of you are seeking work because you are unemployed, while others want to upgrade careers. Employers usually seek to determine whether there is an adequate pool of qualified applicants for a particular job in order to make sound business decisions and plan for the company's growth. As the job applicant, you must also assess the supply and demand of your competition in deciding to accept or decline job offers.

While it may be impossible to peek into a company's résumé file or watch other applicants interview, there are steps you can take to determine how competitive you are and what your niche is. If you do your homework as recommended in this book, you can become confident in knowing how to negotiate your new job, when to decide to accept a job offer, and how to fit into the appropriate companies.

Because you will spend at least half your waking hours at work, it is important to find a place where you will fit in. Approach the job search process as if creating a relationship, so that you will fit in with other employees. Both sides must be happy if the hiring decision is to *take*. From the employer's perspective, this means the search investment pays off, and the workload is completed. Similarly, the employee gets a work identity and regular paycheck. You want to be happy in your work and receive reasonable compensation.

Washington is a town where people tend to rate others on a liberal-versus-conservative scale. Besides just politics, you may have observed how some people tend to gravitate to certain jobs, similar to their own personalities or styles. While this may seem to perpetuate stereotypes or cultural bias, you are the one who has the challenge of creating a relationship with your new employer. People who are happy in their work often have common interests with coworkers.

The second step is to target the right jobs. If you are unsure at this point, an interest test may help identify what occupations you may like, by comparing your interests with people already working in these fields. Aptitude tests can also help you find your talents and skills. Tests to consider include the Strong-Campbell Interest Inventory, Career Assessment Inventory, the Self-Directed Search, General Aptitude Test Battery (GATB), Microcomputer Evaluation and Screening Assessment (MESA), school entrance examinations, and intelligence tests administered by licensed psychologists.

These tests are designed to identify your marketable qualifications in reference to your current skills or with additional training. If you want to obtain a complete evaluation, consult your state's Job Service (see Appendix B), your school's career counseling office, or a private career counseling firm. These resources can provide you with a more focused direction in transferring your skills or seeking training. Government services are free. College career offices usually offer free services for a grace period after graduation, after which they charge a reasonable fee. Private firms generally are the most expensive.

Even with the initial steps worked out, you may still feel somewhat intimidated in trying to find a good employer, so the next step is to assemble your job search packet. You are gearing up to market yourself and you must prepare to address the specific requirements of potential employers. In your plan, decide how much time and funding you can budget for publications, stationery, postage, long-distance calls, transportation, and wardrobe. See Chapter Four for further details on how to assemble your materials.

Once you have organized your job search materials, the next step is to identify and apply for job openings. If you are not working, spend your full-time hours looking for work and, if you can afford it, take some colleagues to lunch. You have the advantage of being able to start immediately in a job vacancy. On the other hand, if you are thinking of changing jobs, you are more attractive to employers because you have a demonstrated success in maintaining a job. Regardless of your current job status, place job-searching as a top priority during your personal time, or others showing more interest will land the job instead of you.

During the boom years of the late 1980s, area companies expanded and recruited many entry-level professionals. Washington got a reputation for being a job-hopping, equity-building transit station. Now, workers tend to keep the jobs they have as many companies have folded or cut back. Managers, experienced professionals, and journeymen alike see first hand how contracts and businesses can dry up, and new graduates anguish over where the jobs are.

Washington employers also enjoy the distinction of having the nation's cream of the crop from which to cull employees. Employers therefore persist in hiring only those with nearly perfect qualifications. In order to learn your niche and compete within this labor market, try to get some tangible feedback from employers after submitting résumés and attending interviews. Such feedback and any offers of immediate employment will tell you where your qualifications are most desirable. Use this feedback in refining your plan.

After developing your plan in written form (see the Summary in this chapter), you will likely relate to one of several career stages for job-searchers: entry-level, experienced professional or tradesman, management, and corporate. Whatever your age or level of education, you will find that Washington is flush with professionals; a lack of laborers is not surprising. There are special considerations for each career category that can help you develop your career path and job search plan.

The First Job

After you have graduated from either high school or college, you have to face the harsh reality of paying your way in life. If you were enterprising and earned your way through school, then you have prepared well for that dream job because you have already experienced some successful interviews. Even if you have been limited to working for class credit or in a family business, you can frame your qualifications competitively. What you have not experienced, you can learn through research and tenacity.

In business, and increasingly in public service, the budget is the meter for making decisions, including hiring. Employers generally expect to "get what they pay for." Management can save money by hiring recent graduates, who will work for less but require some training. On the other hand, employers could save training time by hiring employees who have 3 to 5 years of experience. Your research in identifying appropriate companies who need your skills will be especially valuable here. By applying for jobs with lesser or greater requirements than your qualifications and then examining the results, you can formulate your job targets and better narrow your search to realistic and accessible options.

Whether you seek professional *white-collar* or trade *blue-collar* work as your first job, several principles apply. For one, you have an advantage in marketing yourself as a *quick learner*, a resource for employers to train as they wish. For another, you can also undercut more experienced workers when it comes to salary. No matter what the business, an employer's biggest concerns are whether you will be astute in dealing with clientele and whether you are agreeable to supervision. Entry-level jobs are the ones where you pay your dues, that is, doing all the work people with experience want to avoid.

If you have been wise and obtained job experience related to your chosen field, you already recognize what employers want and can talk about it intelligently. If you feel unprepared in this respect, do your homework on companies before interviewing to learn their objectives and how your qualifications may fit within their frameworks. Practice discussing your abilities in quantifiable terms, that is, specific skills for specific jobs.

Still, to really set yourself apart from other recent graduates, learn to project a polished image. Ask intelligent, but not intimidating, questions; do not appear eager to change things. Be prepared to state your willingness to commit to the company's training program and simply get every aspect of the first impression correct. Have the perfect résumé, application, appearance, etiquette, speech, references, and follow-up technique. Interviewers allow first-timers to be a little nervous, but making basic mistakes may convince an employer that you will make similar miscalculations on the job. If they are going to train you, show them you can follow instructions.

You will learn where to research your specific field and find out about differences among employers in Chapters Two and Three, but the following discussion will focus on general research strategies: consulting those established in your field, reading business periodicals to determine local trends of growth or decline, and practicing interviews with people who serve as your professional references. You can obtain realistic salary ranges, appropriate job titles to target, and names of approachable employers from these same sources.

If you were educated at a nationally recognized institution, you will be more desirable to employers in Washington. If you studied at a community or state college, seek ways to compete on a national level, such as passing national exams, obtaining licenses, participating in professional organizations, and publishing professional articles. Again, emphasize your commitment to the company and your willingness for company training programs.

If someone offers advice, write it down, even if you think it is irrelevant to your career. You may discover it has meaning after more time in the job market. If you follow your employer's rules and complete your assignments, you will likely keep your first job as long as you want, provided you stay within their acceptable salary range. But if you want to achieve promotions, climb the corporate ladder, make meaningful changes in public policy, or otherwise make your presence known, then a long-term plan will help you reach your goals within the established system.

Mid-Career Adjustments

By mid-career in Washington, you may have experienced some success in your work and mastered Metrorail, know where to shop for the right clothing, and driven your parents around the monuments in your new car. At this stage, you and your friends have started families and decorated townhouses. What have you learned on the job? Have you turned your work into a science, where all decision-making is automatic?

If you aspire to promotions, raises, or increased responsibility, look at your employer. Begin to analyze the politics of the company's structure. How do others obtain promotions? What backgrounds do your supervisors have? Does the employer offer tuition assistance? Can a couple of classes provide you with increased technical expertise? If you see improvements to be made or markets to conquer, will an MBA or law degree help you institute your ideas? If so, can you accomplish this with your current employer, or must you find one who specializes in, or encompasses within its larger structure, the departments in which you want to work? Do you work for a firm that features a service or product? Are you a direct part of the production staff or service team? If so, you may want to move into training, inspecting, estimating, supervising, or marketing for your firm.

If you have no experience in these areas, find out if your employer will support you with tuition assistance for more training. If not, seek the training independently and search for a firm that values continued education and career development. Look realistically at your employer; determine if the company has the financial means for growth or promotion from within. Again, if the business is not overly successful, you may want to look elsewhere.

You must resolve these issues in formulating your mid-career plan as they are key to advancement. Beyond knowing what to do, you must know what you want and communicate it. Keep in mind that if you do not upgrade your skills after several years of working on the same job, your employer may take steps to replace you with a less expensive employee.

When approaching your superiors to negotiate advancement, use diplomacy and patience. Emphasize your loyalty and dependability. Remind your supervisor that you make his job easier. A supervisor will never recommend promotion for an employee who threatens to steal his job, but will likely support a valued employee in reasonable advancement. Negotiating will be discussed in more detail in Chapter Five.

If you are part of the support staff of a large company, there is probably a ceiling on your career path. You may move up to a supervisor or department head, but it might happen only through attrition, which could take a long time. Again, look at your employer to see whether the business is solvent and has weathered recent economic trends. A stable company may have more to offer than a small, maverick firm that takes risks. On the other hand, you may wish to gamble with a specialty firm for advancement opportunities or higher salary.

The mid-career point is also a time to look at other aspects of your work life. You may be perfectly satisfied with your professional and financial progress; in fact, you may have earned a respectable reputation and be completely vested in a profit-sharing program. Yet, there are other reasons for considering changing jobs:

- Would you like a more supportive or challenging atmosphere?
- What level of stress or responsibility do you want?
- Do you think you can find a better boss?
- Is there enough hands-on involvement?
- How far is your commute?
- Would you like to travel more?
- Are you interested in perqs, such as a company paid health club membership, tuition, or child care?
- Do you want flexible working hours?
- Would you like to use public transportation?
- Would you like to work in the suburbs?
- Do you want to meet more people through your job? Do you see any possibility for advancement?
- Do you just want a change?

Answer these questions honestly and determine their importance to you. Even one positive answer could be reason enough to look for another job. Keep in mind the issues presented in this chapter and do your research on other employers and your competition. Look at your industry or specialty, together with the difficulty in finding work in your field. It may be you cannot find anything better than what you have, or you could be settling for far less than the labor market offers. If you have developed a relationship with your employer, then you must decide whether to continue, broaden, or conclude that relationship now. If you want to grow, make your plan.

Management and Corporate

After you have amassed the requisite skills and education for this career stage, your employer may require your complete commitment to working as often as needed to keep the business running. This dedication may include being on call, relocating as suggested, following up on customer satisfaction, learning other languages (Japanese, Russian, and Chinese are the current trends), attending social events, or staying every night until you finish the project or close the deal.

Competing at a national or international level is every bit as demanding as what you have ever heard or read, sometimes more. Those responsible for hiring managers or corporate-level employees seek primarily to protect their budget, and look primarily for workers who will increase profits. If you thrive on numbers, adrenaline, networking, and the potential for big money, then this career path is for you. How to break in? It is more than hard work, long hours of data analysis, or power-cocktails. *You must sell your soul.*

Well, what really constitutes a management commitment? The consensus is putting in regular overtime, flattering superiors, implementing ways to make or save the employer money, bringing in big accounts, and superlative public relations. There is little distinction in these areas between garnering upper-level management jobs in for-profit business or public service.

Finding jobs at this level requires substantial research, not unlike the effort needed to succeed once hired. The first place to look is the *Washington Post* Sunday Business section, which has classified ads for upper-level jobs. Two national publications not to be missed are the daily *Wall Street Journal* and its sister publication, the Sunday *National Business Employment Weekly*. Both are available at newsstands. The next steps include following the stock market, networking, researching company financial statistics in the public library, and keeping in regular contact with desirable corporations.

Moving up within government ranks or big business also means developing a network of resources and becoming a helpful resource as well. Networking is not impossible, even if you are new in town. If you have served in the military, join the Reserves. Attend every social function you can. Join organizations catering to your interests (especially those in common with corporate moguls) and participate visibly. Make yourself available to your supervisors for special projects and overtime. For more on networking, see Chapter Three.

There is even more you can do to show your management commitment. For example, concentrate on maintaining state-of-the-art office systems, keeping up with correspondence, ensuring effective staff orientation and continued training, anticipating international economic and political trends, hiring translators, and attending all social occasions for key contacts. Being truly successful here requires a presence of mind and body capable of constant concentration, the force of will to persuade others to follow, as well as the vision to know where to lead. The job must become your life.

What are the rewards for this kind of devotion? If successful, you may enjoy exotic entertainment options, use company expense accounts, meet stimulating people, make big decisions and watch them bear fruit, receive preferential treatment, and generally have all that goes with earning big money. It is up to you to decide whether you have what it takes and how much of your personal life you are willing to sacrifice. If you have done your homework, you are well aware of the niche you qualify for. Keep in mind that most people want the financial and influential advantages, but only a few can take the years of intense work needed to get to the high end of comfort. Even then, your job may not be secure.

Other Career Changes

What do you do when you want to enter a new field, or if you have an unexpected need to look for work? These situations have common elements and special concerns. Both have the anxiety-provoking connotation of starting over, slipping away from ground you have worked hard to attain. Few things sting as hard as losing your identity and livelihood, even if it was by choice.

So let's discuss the worst case first: You have been fired or laid off. Corporate powers have decided to *downsize* and eliminate your position; the project is over and so is your job; or you had a disagreement with the boss and it cost you your job. What now? You have experienced a major blow to your ego, justified or not. If nothing else, you realize your mistake in putting your faith in an employer who was not dependable.

You are now caught in a difficult position between not trusting your judgement when picking employers and needing a job immediately. Give yourself a couple of days to adjust to your new situation. Do something healthy or constructive, something that has worked for you in the past. Ride Rollerblades down the George Washington Parkway biketrail, read an inspiring book, spend the day with your child, or organize your power-sock drawer. Do not take so much time off, however, that you lose your competitive edge.

If you were fired, draw on your anger to fuel your job-searching energy. Do not spend too much time writing critical letters to your previous Personnel office or waiting for the boss to call changing his mind. You have a mission. Contact those individuals whose judgement you trust and ask them to provide a job reference for you.

Unlike references, whom you can pick, the records staffs of previous employers serve to keep simply the statistics of your employment history. Remember, personnel departments of former employers will provide potential employers only with your job title, employment dates, and salary. They usually will not divulge your reason for leaving, job duties, performance evaluations, educational background, your boss' name, or previous employers unless you sign a specific release-of-information form. As you will read in Chapter Four, it is a good idea to contact previous employers to find out what their records indicate about you, before potential employers contact them.

If you are lucky enough to have had some warning about losing your job, take advantage of it. Remember, an employed worker is more attractive to interviewers than one who is not working. If you can look for work before the end of your employment, do it. As you will learn in subsequent chapters, make your job-search plan, research potential employers, prepare your résumé and cover letters, assemble your interview wardrobe, get a haircut, and go for those interviews. Keep in mind that if other similar businesses are downsizing, other stranded employees in your field may be looking for work as well. Competition could be even greater for limited job opportunities, giving you all the more reason to start early.

All is not lost if you do not land that dream job immediately. State law provides for unemployment insurance; you may qualify by being fired or laid off. There are additional stipulations regarding eligibility, and you must apply in the state where you worked. You are also required to seek work to receive benefits. In any case, prepare to spend time in long lines for benefits that last a maximum of 6 months.

If your job search lasts longer than a few months, it is time to amend your plan. If you are spending full-time hours courting potential employers and have received no job offers, analyze your interview or résumé response results. Significant problems at any stage of your search may include wrong job targets, unprofessional or inappropriate correspondence, salary requirements exceeding employers' offers, unattractive telephone manner or appearance, improper interviewing etiquette, or too little/too much follow-up. Have one of your professional references or a career counselor look over your job search materials to provide constructive criticism. Even if painful, such criticism may decrease the distance between you and your dream job.

If it turns out your job target does not exist in the current labor market, maybe a career change is for you. This can be likened to a mid-career adjustment, that is, making a change for nearly the same reasons. It is simply a bigger change that includes not only a different company, location, boss, schedule, or coworkers, but also a new title and less money. The term used for having a salary too high to relinquish is *golden handcuffs*. You may be clever enough to find a new career with great income potential (as will be discussed in the next chapter), but it will likely start at low pay before you make significant gains.

You should adopt special strategies for changing careers. Since your background does not relate directly to your job target (unless you just completed the relevant training), you have to highlight those skills that transfer to the new career. You also should prepare an explanation why you want such a drastic change. Be honest. After all, most people only fantasize about going out on a limb; you are taking action.

Your years of responsible employment may count for something, but essentially you are going to be in the same position as someone applying for his first job. The same rules apply: Emphasize your loyalty and willingness to be trained. Hopefully, since it is a fresh career and you have some work experience, following the rules will not be tedious.

Summary

This chapter has discussed general ideas on formulating your job search plan. Obviously, each person must develop and tailor his own plan. Strategies for accountants and zoo attendants, for example, will differ drastically. This is the format for outlining your job search plan, step by step:

1. Prioritize your goals
   A. Short-term examples: financial, stress, transportation, or scheduling issues
   B. Long-term examples: positive atmosphere, perquisites, professional achievement, commuting distance, social interaction, or advancement

2. Target specific jobs
   A. Outline qualifications (see *Vita* Worksheet, Appendix E)
   B. Consider your preferences about the type of work
   C. Identify the markets you will be monitoring
   D. Limit the geographical area
   D. Identify salary range

3. Assemble resources (see Chapters Three and Four)
   A. Professional quality stationery
   B. Job-specific résumé

C. Cover letter
D. Reference sheet and networking resource list
E. Sample application/SF-171
F. Dependable transportation
G. Appropriate wardrobe
H. Job vacancy publications and other resources (see Appendices A, B, and C)
I. Documentation of your authorization to work in the United States

4. Contact employers (see Chapters Two, Three, and Four, and Appendix D)
   A. Find job leads
   B. Find employers accepting résumés or applications for future openings
   C File applications and résumés

5. Interview with employer (see Chapter Five)
   A. Research employer for work atmosphere and professional reputation
   B. Provide all required information and materials
   C. Attend interview and establish professional relationship
   D. Express desire for job, and learn of decision making plans

6. Follow up with employer (see Chapter Five)
   A. Take notes after interview
   B. Send letter, call, or attend additional interviews as appropriate
   C. Be patient

7. Keep looking!

Chapter Two

THE WASHINGTON LABOR MARKET

Washington presents a wide labor market. Careers are available in just about every field, including health care, legal, engineering, administrative, high-tech, education, accounting, hospitality, retail, and sales. Major employers include the federal, state, and municipal governments; Capitol Hill; law firms; hospitals; universities; utilities; and retail stores. Government consultants and associations occupy a significant section of employers since many have located here, near the federal government. On the other hand, there is relatively little employment in manufacturing. Construction has peaked in this area, as has some of the demand for luxury items and services.

In this chapter, we will examine obtaining employment in all levels of government, and the basics on how to get "Hill" jobs. We will also look at employment issues significant to some key Washington industries, and how they will affect your job search. Finally, the hot Washington careers for the 1990s will be revealed.

The Federal Government

Washington's biggest employer is the federal government. Although Uncle Sam hires in most occupations, the federal government is perhaps the most complex system to enter because of its regulations, paperwork, and competition. The best way to get any federal job is to aim below your qualifications. Once you have achieved government status, you will have preference for better jobs.

There are several ways to obtain federal jobs; all generally require persistence. First, you must identify a viable opening or job announcement. Investigate several avenues in researching vacancy listings: the Federal Job Information Center in the Office of Personnel Management, individual agency or bureau personnel offices, listings in libraries or Job Service offices, calls to recorded joblines (see Appendix B), attendance at job fairs, and subscriptions to some publications (see Appendix A). The Federal Research Service, Inc., is the company whose job listings are most often recommended by federal personnel offices.

It helps to know federal workers who can serve as references and advisors about unadvertised vacancies. Washington is famous for networking; nowhere is this more useful than in the federal government. More often than not, knowing the right person will make the difference in landing you a federal job. The best way to establish or build your personal network is simply to work at maintaining business relationships. Join professional and civic organizations, have lunch across the street from your targeted agency, meet your neighbors, or go jogging on the Mall. And keep a fresh supply of business cards in your pocket.

In applying for a federal position, you must use a Standard Form-171, or SF-171. It is available in federal personnel offices, state job services, and some libraries. As a rule, the federal government neither accepts résumés nor keeps applications on file for future openings. You must apply for specific vacancies, using the vacancy announcement number and filing by the closing date. There are some federal offices excepted from these stipulations.

The Office of Personnel Management (OPM) gives federal jobs one of four classifications: temporary, career-conditional, career, and excepted. Temporary work is often part-time and includes the trades. Career-conditional is employment by an appointment or for a probationary period, which may last up to 1 year. A career, or competitive, position is one in the civilian executive branch; the hiring process must follow OPM's regulations. Excepted employment means the vacancies are excused from these regulations, and applications are filed directly with the agency. Excepted employers include law enforcement agencies, the Federal Reserve System, General Accounting Office, National Security Agency, US Nuclear Regulatory Commission, US Department of State, and the US Postal Service. Lawyers and chaplains are also excepted positions.

OPM requires a background check for all government positions. Because a security clearance is required for some jobs, an existing security clearance is a highly marketable qualification. One way to obtain a background check, which speeds your hiring process, is to volunteer or intern at a federal office. You can then matriculate into a paid position as they become available. It is also a great way to make contacts. United States' citizenship is required for nearly all federal jobs. The laws governing the hiring of aliens are complicated, but the Federal Job Information Center (FJIC) makes available a pamphlet outlining the federal offices authorized to employ noncitizens and the approved countries and occupations.

OPM offers many other services to hasten your government employment, including joblines (see Appendix B); employment seminars for veterans, students, and the public; Administrative Careers with America (entry-level jobs for college graduates or those passing a written exam), and any additional information you need. Call or visit OPM for schedules and announcements regarding these services.

For clerical workers, OPM requires a civil service examination (see FJIC for the schedule). If you qualify for GS-5 and -6 levels with your education or experience, then competency testing may apply regarding the vacancy announcement or federal office where you are applying.

Restructuring and downsizing will likely take place within federal organizations as budget constraints continue. Anyone looking for a job in civilian military and intelligence operations should know that task forces are revising policies and structure with the intent to streamline and combine these missions. As a result, many jobs may be eliminated. Although it will take several years to implement recommendations, applicants with ambitions in these areas must be concerned with downsizing in their long-term job search plans.

If you have government status and want to move up within the federal ranks, stay in regular contact with OPM, or your agency's personnel office, to review job listings. If you have decided on a certain agency or bureau, then contact their personnel department directly for listings. Many find advancement is easier through interagency employment than trying to obtain a promotion from within a single government office. Once you have identified a job announcement, complete an SF-171 and include a Standard Form-50 (SF-50), which is the Notification of Personnel Action confirming your federal employment status. A copy of your last performance appraisal and documents specific to the vacancy are also required.

Municipal and State Government

Local city, county, and state administrations are excellent starting places for your career. They can be stepping-stones to higher government levels or simply opportunities to serve your neighbors in tangible ways. Local governments also tend to be less conservative than the federal government, and therefore, present opportunities for fitting in according to your political preference.

Today many administrations, like their federal counterparts, have budget difficulties and they may experience periodic hiring freezes. Some local government offices, however, will accept applications and résumés to keep on file during such times as well as during normal staffing conditions. Not all jurisdictions are so flexible. Appendix B contains information on available local government joblines and their hiring policies.

No municipal jurisdiction requires US citizenship for employees, except in law enforcement. Montgomery County also requires Maryland citizenship for its police force. Fairfax City, Maryland, and Prince George's County have procedures to give a slight advantage to applicants residing in their respective jurisdictions. The District flatly requires candidates to be residents or provide plans for moving to the city.

Most local governments tend to hire the same kinds of workers— administrators, planners, law enforcement officers, educators, maintenance workers, and human service workers. Depending on the scope and population of the jurisdiction, jobs may be highly specialized. For example, the Commonwealth of Virginia may hire many toll-booth collectors for this area, while College Park, MD, may need only an accountant to provide general financial services. The larger the budget, the greater the need for specialized personnel. You can find employment opportunities with municipal or state offices in nearly every occupational group or industry.

Capitol Hill

Although only a small percentage of the Washington labor force actually works there, Washington is known for the political activities centered on the Hill. The two offices coordinating Congressional employment are operated by the Senate and House of Representatives. If you want to work as a lobbyist, however, you are on your own. The Supreme Court, also on the Hill, provides opportunities for legal and paralegal work. See Appendix B for information on the Senate Placement Office, the House Placement Office, the Supreme Court, and the US Court. Even though there are established channels for job applications, knowing someone who already works on the Hill can give you a definite edge over your competition.

The Senate Placement Office refers résumés of applicants to Senators, Senate personal staff, and Committee offices. Available jobs may include legislative assistant, legislative aide, legislative correspondent, office manager, mail clerk, staff assistant, or other clerical positions. When vacancies occur, the Placement Office is contacted for a list of appropriate applicants. The senator's office will then contact the applicants they wish to interview. Applicants must register in person monthly to remain under consideration.

The House Placement Office serves as an application bank for any Congressional office, including House members and House Committee offices. The office keeps applications for 3 years, but applicants must contact them monthly to remain in their active file. Job vacancies may include receptionist, secretary, legislative assistant, legislative coordinator, schedulist, caseworker, or professional staffer.

If your ambitions focus on lobbying work, there are three common ways to enter the field:

- Start as a legislative aide, advance within the legislative system, and make contacts
- Be a lawyer, perhaps one specializing in regulatory law
- Retire from an influential job in a technical or professional field and then go to work for an association that chooses you for your expertise

The Supreme Court's Personnel Office keeps desirable SF-171 applications on file for one year. Their hiring includes assistant clerk, new case analyst, budget accounting assistant, and ongoing police officer recruitment. The US Court is the level of the federal judiciary system just below the Supreme Court. Their openings may include administration, computers, paralegal, and clerical jobs. Some positions in the judicial branch require a security clearance.

Associations

Associations are excellent resources for finding jobs in various fields, and there are thousands in the Washington metropolitan area. Because organized groups are here to influence national policy, Washington has more associations than any other US city.

In the association world, jobs often can be broken down into three job groups: executive, junior executive, and support. Executive positions include attorneys, accountants, marketers, public relations experts, and others with 7-10 years of work experience. Junior executives serve as coordinators, researchers, or executive assistants, and have a college degree and a few years of experience. Support positions, which may require a few years of technical training or a college degree, include administrative and clerical workers.

Associations in Washington can range from those employing a few in a satellite office (with the home office in another city) to those having thousands of employees. Each association has its own focus. Most can be classified within trade, professional, or nonprofit interest groups.

When hiring workers, associations often look for those with experience in a nonprofit sector or in working with groups. They are interested in applicants with knowledge about their specialty. Many associations seem underfunded. If your qualifications are high and you have significant nonprofit experience working with groups, they may not be able to afford you.

Two excellent resources are available for researching area associations. *Who's Who in Association Management* is the official membership directory for the American Society of Association Executives. This directory can be bought through their society at (202) 626-2758. *The National Trade and Professional Associations of the United States*, published by Columbia Books, Inc., in Washington, DC, is a directory that lists associations by address, size, budget, and contact person; it also cross-references them by location, subject, name, budget, and acronym. Columbia can be reached at (202) 737-3777. Both books are expensive, but you may be able to find them in libraries.

Once you go to work for an association, you may find it difficult to transfer to the *for-profit* arena. Still, there are businesses that have functions similar to association work. Many association professionals also work closely with their industry groups, and so some career mobility is possible.

Engineering

Many professional engineering careers have been devastated by recent economic trends. While electrical and electronic engineers are still in great demand, the market for other specialties has peaked and even disappeared. In the Washington area, most applications are scientific, not commercial. There are some commercial firms in the industrial corridor south of Baltimore, however.

According to Bill Boczany, a recruiter for Source EDP, specializing in engineering personnel services, the market here is driven by a demand for computer software designers. A normal career path for an electrical or electronic engineer is to start in a hands-on position, such as applications; progress to systems analysis; and then rise to departmental management and supervisory positions.

High-technology engineering seems to be the hot job ticket. Recent budget cuts have not significantly affected government contractors for satellites, communications equipment, and some defense hardware, though this may change in the near future. Hardware must be designed and software continually updated to meet the market demands. If you possess these skills, be confident you can find work, though it may take time to move into your ideal job.

Civil engineering, once a field highly recruited and imported into the area, is now in recession. Many large firms and construction companies have reduced their work force or folded altogether. Although the market is tight, mechanical engineers may find work in the maintenance fields, particularly heating, ventilation, and air conditioning (HVAC). There was never a significant demand for industrial, nuclear, or chemical engineers in or around Washington, except with the federal government.

The key to maintaining employment is to stay current with new techniques. For training in state-of-the-art developments, research those employers using such technology and apply for work there. In addition, the Institute for Electrical and Electronics Engineers, (202) 785-0017, offers publications and seminars to aid their members in updating their skills. Some engineers with other specialties might consider returning to college for appropriate coursework. Consider information engineering (the new "IE").

When you consider special résumé techniques, be aware that firms look for your hardware and software qualifications and for your length of experience with each. You will likely be competing directly with computer systems programmers and analysts for these jobs, but relax; in this realm, there seems to be more jobs than workers.

High-tech

According to Carol Covin, author of *Covin's Washington Area Computer Job Guide*, programmers who know C and UNIX can almost write their own job tickets. Results and competence get you noticed in this field. Follow the previous advice and staying current. Today, the following computer qualifications are the most in demand:

- Languages: C and Ada
- Applications software: ORACLE, CASE Tools, IEF, and IEW
- Operating Systems: UNIX, PS/2, and OS/2
- Hardware: DEC, Data General, IBM RS-6000, AT&T B Series, and Sun Workstations

The career path for computer professionals progresses from trainee, programmer, programmer/analyst, and systems analyst to specialized positions for further advancement in areas such as sales, management, network administration, and database administration. Programmers work in two areas: applications and systems. Applications programmers, who are in greater demand in the Washington area, take computer languages and turn them into functional software for their clients. Systems programmers write the computer languages, operating systems, and communications tools the applications professionals use.

The greatest areas of growth for computer professionals are in network communications, workstations, multimedia stations, and imaging. Those who want to become involved in these areas should approach those large companies with the resources to train new employees in the current technology. Training seminars or classes offered by your company are also recommended. To identify such companies, read trade magazines and newspapers, or consult *Covin's Washington Area Computer Job Guide*. Ms. Covin also recommended these strategies:

- Place your software and hardware experience directly under your name in your résumé with the years of experience noted for each area.
- Contact your college career services office to schedule possible interview sessions with recruiters. This strategy is best for recent graduates.
- Review the classified ads one to two months before your anticipated job change. Most jobs advertised are for professionals with three to five years of experience.
- Attend job fairs; research the companies before attending.
- Networking is essential for finding a higher-level job.

Regarding high-tech government contracting, the Department of Defense and many other agencies require a security clearance to work on most contracts; some require polygraph clearances. This process can take six to nine months, which is expensive for the employer. Some government contractors will hire you without the clearance and have you perform nonclassified duties until you are cleared. A current clearance substantially increases your hiring potential.

Consulting

Washington offers what has to be the world's largest collection of consulting firms. Every professional job category discussed in this book can be found in the consulting environment, and while the industry may have peaked in the late 1980s, it is and will remain a major employment source.

Consulting firms are hired by other organizations to work on specialized problems that the organization needs to solve, so that it can concentrate on its primary business. Additionally, consulting firms may help analyze a company's place in the market, the future of the market, or develop new areas for a company to consider.

The federal government is the largest user of private consulting firms, and hires in just about every area of expertise. While everyone thinks immediately of high-tech and computer consulting, the federal government requires specialized studies in education, health care, social services, accounting, affirmative action, job classification, the environment, the arts, legal, transportation, and others.

Private companies in the area also take advantage of the large repository of specialized knowledge found in consulting firms to augment their own specializations. The best source for assignments in the consulting industry is the Sunday *Washington Post* classifieds. However, do not neglect the advertisements in the Sunday Business section, nor your own networking contacts.

Hospitality

A large sector of the hospitality industry is fueled by *blue-collar* workers filling hourly positions. The hospitality industry includes hotels, motels, resorts, furnished professional suites, restaurants, bars, caterers, and private clubs. The local hospitality industry usually hires seasonally to accommodate spring and summer tourists. Since tourism is down, there may be fewer jobs. However, there are still crowds of conventioneers and other paying guests around.

The many graduated levels of hospitality are fixed by the consumers' budget demands. Washington has a generous mix of these demands in all parts of the metropolitan area. Generally, the closer to the White House, the more expensive the establishment offering services. Many Washingtonians work in this area part-time, while others establish this work as their primary career.

Available occupations in the hospitality industry include front desk clerk, concierge, chef, bartender, waitress, baker, housekeeper, manager, maintenance worker, groundskeeper, marketer, doorman, bellman, server, valet, and all types of administrative work. There is potential for specialization within the job classification, depending on the establishment's size.

For jobs that require public contact, an outgoing and accommodating personality is a prime requirement. Professionalism and polish will help you move up within the organization or to a more highly rated enterprise. For management positions, it helps to speak foreign languages—those of guests and employees.

To obtain an entry-level job in the hospitality industry, find someone who already works where you are applying. If you are willing to work as a waiter, for example, ask to work the lunch shift (or one of lesser responsibility). Willingness to work the least demanding shift will help get you hired (meaning a reduced opportunity for tips), and it will allow you to learn the operation. Previous service experience, no matter how brief, is highly desirable. There is a terrible rumor that bending the truth about related experience can get you hired, but if discovered can also get you fired. Be careful of your competition.

Construction and Service

Occupations in these fields run the gamut and are the backbone of the metropolitan area. Washington is laden with highly educated individuals, but there is a great demand for those willing to work in jobs not requiring a college degree.

Most of these jobs pay hourly wages; some require a background of specific training. Many businesses are willing to train inexperienced individuals because the demand for these workers is very high. Positions involving direct service, such as child caretakers, licensed practical nurses, housekeepers, laundry workers, or food service workers, are consistently in demand. Although these jobs are easy to find, they have limited advancement opportunities.

Without formal education, job possibilities decrease. One answer might be working in the security field, as well as several other entry-level careers in demand: courier/delivery, telemarketing, and retail. Maintenance provides some opportunities. The main thing to remember is to keep trying.

Positions in the trades have a graduated career path. An apprenticeship can lead to the job you want. Tradesmen work with their backs and heads. Repairing a car, operating heavy equipment, wiring an alarm, or cutting beefsteaks all require a learning period under a journeyman or master, and you must stay in good physical condition. If you want to become a tradesman, consult someone already working in that field. In some trades, joining a union may increase your chances of obtaining and maintaining employment. Do not, however, depend on this entirely.

These jobs are affected almost daily by happenings in the local economy. For example, the real estate market may dry up, affecting almost everyone—carpenters, asphalt workers, masons, electricians, plumbers, roofers, painters, carpet installers, and pipe layers. When this happened to the Washington metropolitan area in the early 1990s, many tradesmen were faced with significant reductions in their livelihoods. Many, however, transferred their skills into home renovation and associated fields.

Education can increase your placement potential. If you have no high school diploma, consult your county's adult education department for classes and programs to help you obtain your General Equivalency Diploma (GED). Community colleges are another source of realistic, relevant training or education that can pay off quickly. Be sure to investigate whether your class, say in automotive maintenance, can help you compete for jobs and that jobs will in fact be available. Realize that an education, while always a plus, is no guarantee for employment stability.

Health Care

The health care industry is in a state of change because of increased overhead costs as well as the increased cost of insurance. While some are speculating on the future implementation of socialized medicine, the current competition for workers continues between hospitals and private practice. Hospitals operate around the clock, providing workers with economic incentives with shift differentials, while physicians' offices generally offer a more pleasant working environment. The health care field has many specializations and a variety of career paths.

In any situation, physicians run the show, so opportunities for advancement are definitely dependent on further education. Health care decision-makers are conservative. Job applicants should make a conservative presentation. For any specialty, you should have a good assessment of your professional strengths. Be specific about your skills, researching where they are in demand. You can then write a job-specific résumé that gets results.

Hospitals are aggressively recruiting nurses and making working conditions more attractive. Changes include increased salaries, more flexible schedules, and many other benefits. All nursing specializations are in demand, but presently nurses with a chemotherapy background are particularly hard to find.

The general term of "allied health" refers to medical positions other than doctors and nurses. Professional clinicians and therapists, physician assistants, and emergency medical technicians are in great demand. For example, physical therapists are in short supply since many find it a conflict of interest to work directly for physicians. There is also a strong demand from hospitals, which must compete with physical therapy practices for therapists. Other specific opportunities exist for individuals to serve as substance abuse therapists and residential counselors for employee assistance and social service programs.

Janet Cline Patrick, the President of Medical Personnel Services, Inc., said recently that there seems to be a dearth of intelligent, articulate, and pleasant individuals to fill the openings for medical receptionists. Even if you have no background, she says, your gracious personality can win you a job as a medical receptionist.

Other nonclinical positions, such as bookkeeper, appointment scheduler, or file clerk, may require a certain amount of computer literacy and patience for resolving conflicts over the telephone. Medical transcriptionists should have a tolerance for wearing headphones most of the day.

Qualified medical assistants are in great demand as well. There are new Maryland regulations requiring medical assistants to be trained and certified before taking x-ray films. In physicians' labs, technicians must be certified as a Medical Technologist or a Medical Lab Technologist. There is also a short supply of female technicians to do mammograms, as apparently women strongly prefer females for this procedure. The shortage of medical assistants may also be caused by the clinicians' fear of contracting the HIV virus from patients. Whatever your specialty, Ms. Patrick recommends joining a professional association, reading medical periodicals, and attending continuing education classes to keep current in the field and adapt to changes in the industry.

Education

Area public school systems must compete with private schools in recruiting teachers. One nonprofit firm, *Recruiting New Teachers* (see Appendix C), provides information on the teaching profession for teachers, and those who want to become teachers. To obtain a teaching job, they recommend to first obtain a state teaching certification. New teachers must also pass the National Teachers' Exam. Second, file an application with the county or private school system of your choice and then send your résumé to principals of schools where you want to work.

Phil Bigler, a local teacher and author, has several recommendations for teachers applying for work in the Washington area. Knowing teachers who already work in your chosen schools is helpful. Besides knowledge of your subject and possession of a college degree, desirable qualifications for teachers are enthusiasm, flexibility for working within student-centered classrooms, willingness to teach a subject outside your expertise, and knowledge of simulation games. Mr. Bigler also recommends having a genuine desire to help children succeed.

There are alternative certification programs for those who want to enter the teaching profession from other fields. You can register for these programs at George Mason University, American University, and George Washington University. The teaching field is one where continued education is a lifelong process. Advancement beyond teaching requires more specialized education in administration or in counseling and guidance.

To find new employment, *Recruiting New Teachers* lists *The AS-CUS Annual: A Job Search Handbook for Educators*, from the Association for School, College, and University Staffing. It has articles and advice on job seeking skills. ASCUS can be reached at (708) 864-1999. Mr. Bigler recommends the periodical, *Education Week*, as a good resource for administrative vacancies as well as some teaching positions.

Having a master's degree increases your income potential in all jurisdictions; however, it may decrease your placement potential as school hiring officers may favor applicants with lower salary expectations. Secondary education offers better salaries.

Currently, the District recruits teachers continuously and pays the highest salaries. Other jurisdictions may not have as high a demand, but Prince William County is growing, Prince George's County is diverse, and Fairfax and Montgomery Counties have large populations to support. All salaries in this area are very competitive on the national scale. For the future, Mr. Bigler expects the teaching labor market to improve after 1993 when the baby boomers' children (the echo) settle into secondary education.

In choosing a school, you should be aware that private schools in the area tend to have smaller classes and better working conditions, but they offer lower salaries and fewer benefits. There is a wealth of private schools and alternative learning centers in the area, which may offer teaching jobs. Find them in the telephone book yellow pages under "Schools."

Another area of the education market, college-level teaching, is significantly different. A doctorate is usually required, the competition is great, and turnover is low in college positions. Teachers may be interested in the hidden market in Washington for professionals to teach one class in the evenings at colleges and universities. Contact college department heads with your proposal to teach a class on an enrollment basis. Community colleges seem the most open to this arrangement. As with all college teaching, your credentials and publications mean more than your teaching skills.

Journalism

College professors are not the only ones who publish. For some, publishing is a lifestyle. Journalists play an important part in maintaining the checks and balances inherent in this country's Constitution and Bill of Rights; they chase and report stories every day. Journalists work in both print media and broadcasting. Both groups can engage in cutthroat competition, and both suffer in an economic slump when advertising revenue declines. Many do not survive the subsequent budget cuts.

Hatim Heymar, an executive for the National Association of Broadcasters (NAB), is somewhat discouraging about finding journalistic work; he admits that often finding work is a case of being in the right place at the right time. He reports Washington is rated ninth in Area-Dominated Influence (ADI), which is a method of analyzing the nation's news markets. He adds that most professional journalists start in smaller markets (below 20 ADI) to gain experience and then move up to assistant positions in Washington or other major markets. Just being near Washington, however, can make a difference in getting a job here. When openings occur, station managers want them filled immediately, and local applicants therefore have the advantage. The main market here includes four network and two independent television stations (see Appendix C) and three main news radio stations (WTOP, WMAL, and WRC). NAB operates a jobline (see Appendix C), breaking down occupations within the field to talent, sales, production, engineering, and reporting.

Mr. Heymar states the news business hiring can be very subjective; it helps to have your armor ready in case of rejection. He advises not to rule out radio when planning your career and offers these additional job searching techniques: join broadcasting associations for conventions and publications; never stop networking to stay fully informed of any job openings; and hire an agent.

If you seek to become a staff member at any of the area's major periodicals, there are several angles. Intern for free, and gain professional experience and contacts; bid for and submit ideas for freelance articles; demonstrate success on a local newspaper level; and seek informational interviews for specific feedback on how your qualifications rate. Major print media companies include the *Washington Post,* the *Washington Times,* the *Washingtonian, New Republic, US News and World Report,* and the Gannett Company which includes *USA Today.*

One way to establish a professional reputation as a writer or reporter is to clamor for any free-lance assignment you can find. Freelancing requires much networking and assistance from various writers' groups. Washington Independent Writers, at (202) 347-4973, provides job listings for members. Writing advertising copy and working on the Hill are other ways to build your qualifications. Professional associations and government agencies generally print newsletters and journals, which need editors and technical writers.

Law Enforcement

Becoming a police officer or government agent requires thorough training on investigative techniques, safety and apprehension, firearms, and the law. Police officers serve at every jurisdictional level. Qualifications for positions in law enforcement include US citizenship, successful completion of written and physical examinations, a battery of interviews, and thorough background checks. To move into federal rank, a military or local law enforcement background can be highly desirable. If you seek a career in law enforcement, you need to communicate your reasons honestly and clearly. The recruiter can then point you toward the branch or field most in line with your objectives. This is a lifestyle, not a job; you must make sure you are content with your commitment.

Federal law enforcement agencies include the Federal Bureau of Investigation, the Drug Enforcement Administration, the Central Intelligence Agency, the US Customs Service, the US Marshals' Service, the Secret Service, the Capitol Police, and the Bureau of Alcohol, Tobacco, and Firearms. The military also offers civilian law enforcement, criminal investigation, and security positions. Civilian positions exist within all law enforcement agencies. For example within the Justice Department, there is a great demand for intelligence analysts and diversion investigators, whose duties include looking into ancillary products and services used by individuals breaking specific laws.

There also is a great demand for municipal law enforcement officers, especially in the Washington area. Relatively high rates of violent and white-collar crime strain the local ranks. Local groups therefore have to compete with the federal agencies to attract bright and ambitious candidates. Whatever your objectives for working in law enforcement, you can likely find them in the Washington metropolitan area.

Legal

The newspapers are full of articles about the lawyer glut, and you should know that Washington has more lawyers per capita than any other American city. For help in finding a legal job, obtain the directory published by the National Association of Law Placement [(202) 667-1666]. This directory lists legal employers, cross-referencing them by subject and location. The key is to contact each targeted firm to find out firsthand what qualifications, interests, and philosophies they seek. This effort will be considerable, but it will get you noticed. Law firms, more than most other businesses, look for commitment.

Janet T. Roy, Chairperson of the National Capital Area Paralegal Association (NCAPA), reports that working as a paralegal is the career of the 1990s. She defines two career tracks for paralegals: one for college students or graduates spending a few years in the legal field before entering graduate school and the other for career paralegals, who may not be as well-educated but represent a more stable hiring population.

College paralegals often request assignments to litigation departments and case clerk positions. On the other hand, career legal assistants make a commitment to be trained to the firm's operations and then take assignments as permanent parts of specialized legal teams. With the cost of retraining college paralegals every two years increasing, firms now are looking for career legal assistants to be groomed into professional legals specializing in specific areas of the law. They are less expensive than lawyers but perform many of the same functions. This arrangement leaves the law firm free to assign its lawyers as casework supervisors, thus saving the firm money by reducing the need to hire lawyers.

For those interested in obtaining a paralegal position, Ms. Roy recommends having *flawless* job search documents, since law firms expect your work as a paralegal to be completely professional and error-free. Your résumé should focus on your experience and specialty as related to the firm's needs. Communication, writing, dealing with people, patience, persistence, attention to detail, and skill in negotiations among attorneys, staff, and clients are all keys to success. These capabilities must be demonstrated during the interview.

Paralegal specialties in demand include environmental, international (being bilingual gives you a definite edge), litigation, bankruptcy, corporate, financial (especially "Blue Sky" securities and exchange laws), and government. NCAPA publishes job listings for its members. The American Bar Association also has job descriptions for review to give you a better idea of what to expect.

Financial

Jobs related to money are as tight as Congress' debts are big. Not only have banks suffered through the recent recession, but investment consultants, insurance companies, mortgage firms, and real estate associates have had to struggle to survive.

The banking industry is known for its detail, such as dotting every "i" and accounting for every penny. According to an official with the American Bankers' Association, the local banking industry is "terrible." He recommends that those aspiring to banking careers should move to the midwest. Nearly all area financial institutions are downsizing; many banks are looking to merge with other banks to combine departments and lay off extra staff.

Working for the government is one alternative to relocating if your present job in the financial area has been cut. As banks and savings and loans fail, the work for government financial regulatory offices picks up. Consequently, the Federal Deposit Insurance Corporation and the Resolution Trust Corporation (see Appendix B) are recruiting financial and legal professionals to assist in their regulatory work.

Another effect of the area recession for the financial industry is that many private firms are hiring accountants and financial analysts to assist them in streamlining their operations and reducing costs. Since competition is strong, your best strategy is to present a complete, professional, and conservative image, as well as a stable work history. Certification is usually required to maintain employment. If your job was eliminated, look for ways to transfer your skills into policing the industry or lowering a company's overall costs.

Sales

In Washington today, there is a vast spectrum of goods and services sold at every economic level. If you are thinking of finding a sales position, think first of selling what you like to buy. Chances are you will have a special expertise or product knowledge you can offer the employer, and you can obtain discounts on your purchases as well. On the other hand, if you have developed a high level of expertise in your field, you may seek to move into marketing or sales of your firm's product or service.

First of all, you have to be prepared to sell your personality to obtain a sales position. Those jobs offering serious money are staffed by those working on commission. Do not neglect benefits, however, in negotiating your contract. Also, for high-level product sales jobs, be prepared to be asked about your credit rating. Refusing this information appears to them that you have something to hide. It is a good idea to request your credit rating on your own before applying for jobs to see if there are any errors. While waiting for the report, research the merchants or firms for whom you wish to work and determine their level of success. This information should be available at the library or Chamber of Commerce.

If you are interested in a sales career, know that the one quality for advancement is financial results. The numbers will get you the executive positions. Make sure you do not neglect your commission arrangements once you move up. Also, if you supervise people and are responsible for their effectiveness, negotiate a portion of their commissions.

Administrative/Clerical

There is a great demand for those to fill administrative and clerical jobs in Washington. If your skills are not competitive, however, you will not keep the job for long. Washington has the apparent distinction of having the largest market of secretaries with college degrees, who are all waiting for jobs to open within their expertise. Consequently, there is a high turnover rate.

Employers hire administrative workers to attend to the regular details of everyday business and to allow technicians and specialists to produce the goods or provide the services of the company. Administrators deal with coordinating personnel, time, supplies, equipment, and funds; pushing papers; and resolving problems. Common occupations include human resources generalist, accountant, inventory manager, file clerk, and scheduling manager.

A telephone company official offered this advice to administrative workers. He projected that, because of area downsizing and budget cuts in all industries, the administrative/clerical job market will be saturated with highly qualified applicants who do not wish to leave the area. He termed the current situation a "hirer's market." Since there is a significant decline in the availability of jobs beyond the $35,000 level in all industries, you should specialize your interests and administrative skills to increase your income potential. Target your qualifications to employers who share your focus.

Do not rely on answering classified ads to find administrative jobs. There is too much competition, and your résumé will be lost in the avalanche of applicants. Target the firms where your skills apply; make cold calls to determine their hiring schedules and policies. Chances are they have regular openings.

Independent Consulting

It takes about three times the effort of job-searching and networking to obtain consulting work. You must have connections. Networking at this level is similar to developing a huge list of professional references and then seeking work from them. Connections lead to more connections. Although your initial attempts may not be successful, second- or third-hand referrals may work.

If you are new in town and have limited networking possibilities, or if you just want to expand your contacts, check the local library for directories of industry, business, or agencies in your specialty. Also, socializing can help, but do not depend on it entirely. Remember, schmoozing is secondary to competence.

After you have a list, say, of at least 100 firms, make telephone call upon call. The object is to obtain a meeting where you can pitch your services in a matter of minutes. Promise busy executives to keep the meeting short and convince them that your services will free them to attend to other sides of the business. Do not be shy in presenting yourself; this is your livelihood. When sending correspondence to prospective clients, use matching professional-quality business cards, letterhead, personal notecards, and perhaps brochures of your services. Depending on your specialty, you may also want to have a portfolio of your work.

If an executive cannot use your services, ask him to refer you to other firms or hiring officers who may contract to professionals like you. Add these names to your list with the person who provided them to you. When calling the referral, let him know who referred you there.

Always send a thank-you letter to people you contact on the telephone; include your résumé for their reference. Let them know when you will be calling again and never miss the call. Keep a log or record of each contact, and note your impressions of them after every call or meeting. Even though nine out of ten people will not use your services, you can still maintain professional relationships with them. A good rule of thumb is to check with each contact every two weeks to a month.

When you obtain a meeting with a prospective client, treat it like an interview. Your pitch cannot sound canned; if it does, it will offend the executive. Keep in mind the employer's needs and frame your most recent projects in terms of how they relate to the client's current objectives. Call this your two-minute résumé. If the meeting does not result in an immediate assignment, request permission to submit a proposal to resolve some difficulty currently experienced by the firm. Ask for the executive's frank opinion and ensure your complete confidentiality in this regard. After the meeting, send a follow-up letter confirming the events and arrangements.

Independent consulting can occur in practically any field, and often the money can sound attractive. Remember, however, you will have to provide your own insurance, do your own selling, and run your own administrative errands. You will often be the first cut when times are tough and one of the last called when times improve. It is not a career path for everyone.

The Hot Careers

Finally, as promised, here is a short and noninclusive list of the hot careers in Washington. These jobs can be entered quickly with perhaps six months of specialty training if you are in a related field. Having the right talent will connect you with jobs providing a quick payoff.

The biggest payoff, perhaps, is in sales in practically every industry. Professional firms also may hire marketers to drum up business. A few years ago, real estate and stock market sales might have topped the list, but these businesses are definitely downsizing in a slow economy.

Nursing is a field that is wide open. All disciplines, entry-level to top administrative, are in demand. Salaries jumped exponentially in the 1980s, and your continued education could increase your income potential.

There are other hot jobs besides sales and nursing. If you have a computer programming background, learn the C language to advance your career. Besides programming, any firm having high-technology equipment will need someone to repair it, and the starting salaries for high-tech maintenance are better than average. Paralegals and physician assistants also have respectable starting salaries, but there is little advancement without further education.

While some may argue that parenting is the most significant Washington career, livelihood and salary are the objects here. So the truly hottest career is the one you like going to every day. Jobs come and go, so try to find one you will enjoy.

Chapter Three

FINDING THE JOBS

Now that you have selected your career path and know roughly the niche you seek, you are ready to look for job openings. This is more than coupon clipping for a workplace. Depending on your immediate needs, you want to see the whole labor market to identify those "best-fit" companies.

The bulk of your research work will be spent in this phase, and it can be the most daunting. You are opening yourself and your professional reputation to unfamiliar territory. Whether the job is advertised or not, employers are in a position of control in deciding whether to hire you. You are the one circulating your résumé, beating the pavement, and telephoning. Be aware some employers may network to find out about you and where you have also applied, even while you investigate them.

In your quest to create and develop a relationship with a new employer, finding the job opening can be compared to determining if the employer is "available" to hire. Make the employer feel singled out as desirable to work for, not just another factory with a check-writing department. Even if you have sent out 150 résumés in the metro area, make each cover letter seem like it is the only one you have sent.

Keep a job search notebook to organize your information about each company so you can provide them immediate and personal attention. A general framework for recording employer information (copies of this in Appendix D) is on the next page.

Make sure you obtain thorough information as follows:
- Complete address including zip code (nine digits if the employer uses the additional four)
- Correct spelling of address and contact person's name

Employer: _____

Address: _____ Phone: (____) _____

_____ Contact: _____

Openings: (note location, vacancy announcement numbers, salaries,

closing dates, etc.)

_____

Application recommendations: _____

Date Applied: _____

Interview: _____

Follow-up: _____

Notes: _____

_____

- Extra names of the hiring officer, interviewer, supervisor, or other key contacts in the hiring process
- All of contacts' genders and titles
- Exact job title of the vacancy
- Employer's preference for applications, résumés, or walk-in interviews.

There are many ways to find jobs other than perusing the classified advertisements. You can spend your free time researching all available employers, or you can look until you find something good enough. It is up to you. Washington is a small town in many ways; it can consume those expecting to rise too quickly or outside the established ranks. A slow news day has ruined more than one career. Yet, it is large enough to offer many opportunities for the ambitious.

In beginning your job search strategy, decide on your immediate versus future needs. If you want to find a job tomorrow, several methods apply: the classified ads, job fairs, joblines, job and sign postings, career services, and some short-term cold calling. If you are researching the market for a job upgrade, there are several additional ways to round out your efforts, which include more comprehensive cold calling; networking; using temporary, volunteer, or internship experience; or starting your own business. The most familiar job search technique of course, is using the "want ads," or classified advertisements.

Classified Ads

With pages and pages of classified newspaper ads, you must read every tiny job title to find just a few to pique your interest. Millions of other applicants also read the same ads you do. Your hands get dirty, your eyes get tired, and your get shoulders tense. It becomes a ritual, especially on Sunday. In spite of some tedious aspects, the classified ads are a valuable resource. They are also an excellent way to find out about career-related events, such as job fairs.

For the metropolitan area, the *Washington Post* is the chief source of job advertisements. To cover your bases, however, check also the *Washington Times* and the county *Journal* newspapers. For upper-level jobs, check also the *Post* Sunday Business section, the Sunday *National Business Employment Weekly*, and the daily *Wall Street Journal*. Visit a newsstand or convenience store to look for local newspapers, free circulars, and other publications providing job listings for government or specific locales. Check to see which weekday the papers, specifically the employment sections, "hit the stands." Consider subscribing to those publications useful in your job search. You can take heart in your search that most of your competitors will rely chiefly on the ads. Do not neglect the classifieds, but also consider other strategies and sources.

One common mistake among job searchers is to look only under one or two job titles for listings, instead of reading the entire section. You may find administrative ads listed within many different industries; simple misprints can place headings away from their counterparts. Job titles are not carved in stone.

It is usually best to circle listings, instead of cutting them out, because you might cut your dream job on the other side! After reviewing the whole section, you may want to clip the ads you have answered and save them in your job search notebook.

Also read "between the lines" of the ad; notice what an employer does not say. His strategy may be as simple as trying to save money on the ad, but you should think about what he may be hiding. Some may use "blind" ads, which request your response to a post office box. Such employers may not want their business competitors or their own personnel to know they are hiring. Also, they may not want to spend time on inquiry calls or rejection letters.

An ad omitting the company name and listing only a telephone number forces you to contact them only by telephone; they usually consider your call as a first interview. If the hiring officer does not like the way you sound, he may say the job is filled. If the ad does not list a telephone number, they probably do not want to receive calls. A brief call is still acceptable to confirm complete information.

Beware of ads promising great financial reward without describing the actual job duties. These jobs are usually sales positions and are not for everyone. Any employer trying to trick people into accepting jobs is probably hiding something; you do not want to find out after you have started work there. Beware also of employers whose receptionist does not identify the company's name; these may be disreputable businesses.

Job Fairs

Job fairs can be specific to an industry or employer. They are efficient resources for job-seekers and hiring officers, and they lend an intensity to competition. Look for them at hotels, colleges, and convention centers. Use these opportunities to examine other job-seekers, seeing how your first impression compares to theirs.

The federal government has several job fairs throughout the year. Refer to the Federal Job Information Center (see Appendix B) for scheduling. Get in line early in the morning. (Do not camp out the night before, as it will ruin your suit.) Waiting lines routinely extend outside the location. Take many copies of your SF-171 and résumé because some offices accept both.

One way to prepare for job fairs is to obtain a listing of participating employers before the fair. If you obtain the list beforehand, call them to see if they are hiring in your field. You may also obtain company pamphlets or other information in this way. At the job fair, focus on the employers you have targeted.

Joblines

Another way to review regular listings is to call employers' joblines. These are telephone numbers equipped with recordings of available jobs, or at least outlining application procedures. Jobline directories are available in this book's appendices; municipal and federal government joblines are contained in Appendix B, and private employers' joblines are contained in Appendix C. Since people with hearing impairments cannot listen to joblines, TDD numbers (with access to a telecommunications device for the deaf) are provided if available. Some federal agencies list vacancies primarily through their joblines. Joblines have several advantages:

- They are operational 24 hours a day
- Employers using them are generally large enough to have regular openings
- You can contact the employer silently, even while at work
- You do not have to identify yourself until you choose to apply

When calling joblines, take notes in your job search notebook. Find out what day of the week and how often personnel offices update their joblines to ensure you that you learn of job openings as soon as possible. Bring a fund of patience for listening; joblines may run for as many as ten minutes before you hear about a job you want. Stay alert so you do not miss the vacancy announcement number and have to listen again.

The general trend is for joblines to be operated by touch-tone operated. Touch-tone calling allows more people to call simultaneously and access specific job targets more quickly. Do not let busy signals discourage you; call on evenings or weekends. If the jobline recording is not easily understood, call the personnel department for more information. Note, however, that if you decide to call personnel directly to see if they are hiring in your field, they will likely refer you to the jobline anyway since it is designed to save them time.

Job Postings

Another personnel timesaver for employers is to post job listings in their offices, where you can visit to review them. This may be inconvenient, so some companies will mail you job bulletins. Some postings include job descriptions; others make them available separately.

Other sources of job postings include local job service offices, public libraries, chambers of commerce, public notice boards, professional associations, and college career services. Consult the blue pages of your telephone directory for job services, public libraries, and chambers of commerce. College instructors, high-level management, or directories in Appendix A can direct you to appropriate professional associations, which generally require membership before providing job referrals. College career offices usually limit their services to alumni and students. You may also find public postings in churches, hospitals, supermarkets, malls, community associations, or clubhouses.

Sign Postings

Many retailers, hospitality merchants, mass manufacturers, and construction companies advertise their employment needs in their windows. If you want a job, drive around the neighborhood. You may find work just by walking through an industrial park or mall. Prepare to interview immediately and perhaps start work. Employers posting these kinds of listings are significantly shorthanded; once they find suitable employees, they stop looking.

Career Services

Public and private career services can help you prepare for job searching and can provide job leads. Many local governments provide career counseling offices (as well as job service offices), which are excellent sources for employment support groups or job search training classes. Local Job Service offices provide similar services.

Private (for profit) career services charge a fee, either to the employer or the applicant. If the employer pays the firm to fill a vacancy, the firm is classified as a "headhunter." The representative will encourage you to interview with an employer; if you accept the job, then he will get paid. If you pay the fee, then you expect the firm to look for a job you want. The fee is usually a percentage of your salary, or it could be a fixed service fee. In any event, it may be a good idea to have someone else review the contract before signing. Remember, however you get the interview, it is you who will be responsible for getting the job offer.

Some firms specialize in specific industries and may be more knowledgeable about career paths. You may find private career coun-

seling firms in the yellow pages of your telephone directory under
Career and Vocational Counseling, Management Consultants, Personnel Consultants, and Employment Agencies. Look under another
heading, Résumé Service, to find firms that may also provide job-
seeking skills training and job leads.

Using these services saves you time. If you rely on them exclusively,
however, you could restrict your look significantly at what the labor
market offers. For a really comprehensive look, you must do a labor
market survey by cold calling.

Cold Calling

Cold calling is similar to door-to-door sales, just like it sounds, but
you must keep in mind that you are the product, not brushes or
vacuums. First, you must first target your group of employers by
defining the variables in your research. Consider what you want in
location, industry, employer size, or other qualities. Next, pull out
the telephone book.

If you are limiting your research to a specific industry, look for
headings in the yellow pages where employers may hire your targeted
job or career path. For instance, journalism majors should look under
Newspapers, News Publications, News Service, Magazine Publish-
ers, Radio Stations, Television Stations, and Writers—Business. Job
titles, such as accountants or receptionists, may be difficult to cate-
gorize under a few headings because they are administrative and
used in all industries. When in doubt, consult the yellow pages index
but do not neglect the blue pages for government listings.

You also can limit your search within yellow pages headings by
location. Look for targeted towns or streets in the addresses listed
and highlight them. If you want to search for a company in a specific
jurisdiction, contact the county or town Chamber of Commerce,
which will have a listing of its members.

If you have decided you want to work for the federal government
in any federal office, locate the directories of every personnel office
available from community resources. Consult a library or contact
Federal Reports [(202) 393-3311] for a directory of personnel offices. From this directory, you can cold call every office or narrow
the scope of your job target or location.

If you want to work for a large company, any large company, you
can browse the public library for several references providing employee totals for Washington area employers. *Dun's Regional Busi-*

ness Directory, Lead Source, the Business List Source for Northern Virginia, and *Washington DC Marketing Directory* (for the District and surrounding Maryland suburbs) are some of the better ones. The library is also a great source of directories for businesses in manufacturing and industry. *The Virginia Industrial Directory, The Northern Virginia Marketing Directory, The Virginia Business Directory,* and *The Maryland Manufacturing Directory* have sections listing companies by industry. These lists are more detailed than yellow pages headings. Also, Fairfax County Public Libraries have a guide for using the county library resources for job hunting. Consult a reference librarian with your specific needs.

Once you have identified appropriate employers, you are ready to start telephoning. Cold calling is an art, unpredictable and discouraging, but just as important as interviewing to the job searcher. Asking meaningful questions and keeping thorough records are the keys to success here. These records become the foundation of your job search notebook.

In cold calling, prepare your voice first. Start your conversation with an optimistic tone, be polite, and accommodate the instructions of the person fielding your call. Remember, he has the authority to direct your call to the correct person. Many callers think themselves savvy enough to form an immediate alliance with the receptionist; this approach usually comes across as fake. It takes several calls and visits to establish rapport with the receptionist or hiring officer.

Always identify yourself at the beginning of your call. Even if the person answering does not immediately record your name, he will provide you more information and trust you more easily. Evidently, there must be a significant amount of telephone misrepresentation in Washington. It may be easy to provide another name to protect your anonymity, but it is very easy for the employer to identify a résumé and cover letter that included information discussed over the telephone. Create your relationship with them on honest ground.

After identifying yourself, state the purpose of your call in polite, businesslike terms. Generally, if you want information about the types of jobs available, ask for personnel or the employment office. If the company is small, the receptionist may have the information or will direct you to a manager or owner. This is not the intimidating, agonizing process you think it is. People call about jobs every day.

When calling, have your format ready to take notes. Always follow the employer's application procedure. (As you will learn in Chapter Four, there are additional strategies to accelerate the process and draw positive attention to your application.) Have your *vita* worksheet (see Appendix E) in front of you for immediate reference in case an employer has questions. You also can make notes for modifying a résumé according to the employer's specific requirements.

Cold Calling for Future Openings

If you do not find any immediate openings on some of your cold calls, ask if companies keep résumés or applications on file for the future. Follow their procedure for this as well. Résumé and application submission are discussed in Chapter Four, and there are special considerations for those to be kept on file. Your cover letter, which should always be submitted with your résumé, should be geared to your desire to be contacted when openings occur. You would like to have a "standing offer" to interview at their convenience.

Find out how long they keep these files active and renew yours accordingly. If you really want to work there, call them every month or so to check on job vacancies. Learn to ask specifically for someone in the personnel department. Make sure this person ranks high enough to influence the hiring decision but low enough to take calls regularly. You can determine this most effectively in person by observing the personnel staff.

It is most important in making cold calls to thank the person on the other end of the line for his time spent providing you with assistance and information. If that person is a little less than polite, you can imagine the kind of impatient, arrogant, demanding, or otherwise puffed-up people who have called before you. You can be the applicant who makes the personnel staffer or receptionist relax and enjoy his job.

If you have advanced by cold calling through the company's channels to the point where a hiring officer has evaluated your qualifications (by telephone or application), and he does not think you qualify for work there, ask for referrals to other employers more appropriate for you. Respect his opinion and do not resent his frankness. You can then use his name as a "built-in" reference in contacting the new company.

Networking

For many Washingtonians, networking is the most practiced skill of job searching. Many use it after they are hired for getting business. Corporate types have their plastic-encased business card files, college graduates have their alumni chapters, journeymen have unions, and clergymen have the church. You probably have more available resources than you realize.

Chances for networking occur every day. Consider these opportunities: where you shop, exercise, dine, attend church, get your car fixed, or spend your free time. In addition, former employers, family, friends, club members, or public servants function as arteries to others who may have relevant information.

An excellent strategy is to contact social service organizations or review the calendar in the business section of newspapers for employment support groups. Some resources specialize in specific populations, such as those of advanced age, women reentering the work force, those with English as a second language, or others in specific occupations. Members of these groups may come and go, but all share common ground. Such organizations are supportive forums providing realistic feedback on your job search experiences.

If you truly know no one in Washington, get busy. Join professional associations and attend the meetings. There is an unlimited supply of hobby and personal interest groups here, especially in politics, so join one or two. If you have children, they offer many opportunities to meet other area parents. Just in the business of living here, you need a doctor, dentist, home, transportation, and personal items. In getting to know the area, ask around about who the good employers are. Most people will have some opinion.

It is not dishonorable to be looking for work. Let people know! Be ready to provide them specific ways for how they can easily help you. Thank them for their help with a short letter describing your job targets; include your résumé so they can discuss your qualifications intelligently with others. After sending them this information, call after about ten days to follow up on their findings and thank them for their efforts. Heed their recommendations and report your findings. Build your network and, when you have found your dream job, throw a party. Everyone attending can network for themselves.

Advertise Yourself

Advertising yourself in a newspaper is not a recommended method. The Washington work climate is reputable enough so that employers can let applicants come to them. If employers seek you, it will be on your professional reputation. Advertising appears desperate.

On the other hand, there may be specific situations where your skills are so focused that you cannot identify any employers who would have a job in your specialty, let alone an opening. Advertising may work here, but use it only as a last resort. You can best use this technique in professional publications.

Temporary Work

Temporary work is an excellent way to get an overview of the labor market, discover inside information on employers, and build your network; however, it is emotionally draining to have frequent changes in employer, location, schedule, business procedures, and coworkers. If you are competent in your field and you find a temporary service to coordinate your hiring, look on this as an option to bolster your budget until you find a permanent position.

As with private placement firms, take care to review the temporary agency's contract carefully; perhaps have someone else read it as well. Some companies require specific commitments over time, while others may require you to accept a certain ratio of job arrangements to maintain your contract. Shop around for salaries and benefits; there is likely a demand for temporary workers, especially in data processing and administrative fields.

Working as a consultant can be another option for temporary work. Depending on your profession, you can find consulting opportunities by networking. Consulting gives the applicant and employer a chance to examine the other without making a permanent commitment, while still filling immediate needs for both. The lack of benefits is one drawback, but salaries are generally higher. For more information, see the previous chapter.

Volunteer Work/Internships

Another way of parlaying your skills into a permanent position is to volunteer. This is not appropriate for all occupations, but it is common in fields related to creativity and social change. It can be highly effective if you are entering the workforce or changing careers, and your skills are not competitive.

Arranging a volunteer or internship assignment is very similar to finding paid positions. It is most effective, however, if you have a professional referral from a teacher, colleague, or other associate in order to be taken seriously by the employer. The Peace Corps is an excellent source for gaining professional skills through volunteering, especially when you consider the trends toward international markets and exchange.

Common volunteer jobs in Washington include social service positions, museum docents, broadcasting interns, activists, campaign volunteers, and recycling coordinators. Any on-the-job training arrangement is similar, such as Job Corps or apprenticeships. Local governments have long lists of social services accepting volunteers. Hobbies or personal interests may be a possible new career.

Self-employment/Small Business

You probably do not have the luxury of trying a job without a paycheck. In addition, you may not tolerate management policies or working exclusively at a desk. Working for yourself may be the career you seek.

It is a good idea to have some business or management experience before attempting a financial venture, but you are not alone. The Small Business Administration (see Appendix B) is available for any information you may need; bookstores and libraries also offer advice. Plan on attending the Washington Convention Center's yearly meeting for franchising businesses. Consult an attorney before presenting your business plan for a loan approval.

Summary

If you have come this far, you have already done excellent research in finding out what is available to you in the Washington area. The next step is to prepare your job search materials. Looking for work is a full-time job. Your job search notebook should grow every day. You probably have developed favorite employers, and it is time to make contact.

Chapter Four

CONTACTING THE EMPLOYER

After you start your research, you may find several employers with openings of interest. What next? The answer is to keep going *One More Step*. While getting the job entails finding the opening, contacting the employer, filing the application, interviewing, and following up, you can turn from simply going through the motions to an effective and successful job campaign. You do this by showing your interest and working within the employer's established structure.

After finding the opening, your next step is to contact the employer directly. As you learned in Chapter Three, you must accommodate the person answering the telephone, and whoever may be advising prospective applicants of résumé submission rules. Be polite and follow their instructions. You can assert yourself, however, by asking to go *One More Step* until receiving a polite "no." When telephoning, get up early! You are competing with the rest of Washington.

Examine the five steps in the job search process; each is a progression toward your goal of a job offer. At each step, you can request to proceed to the next. You advance according to your assertiveness, and within the employer's parameters. Here are some examples of using the *One More Step* method:

1. Finding the Opening. Unless an advertisement says, "no phone calls," find the telephone number and call the personnel department or hiring officer of the company. Do not be too timid to call information or search the telephone book. The first step is to ask their procedure for submitting résumés or applications.

2. Contact. Obtain the complete mailing address, hiring officer's name and gender, and request a job description if one is available. The next step is to ask whether the résumé can be delivered in person or by fax. If the answer is no, then mail it. If yes, then fax it within the hour (also send a hard copy by mail) or deliver it by the next morning. The next step is to determine whether the employer requires an application and additional documentation, and whether you may "drop by" the office to take care of this.

3. Application. Dress ready to interview. Complete their forms and provide other documents while inside the office. This is an excellent chance to gauge the atmosphere, whether other employees enjoy working there, and what the general dress code is. The next step is to ask if they are scheduling interviews, and if it is possible to interview that day since you are already there. If the answer is no, thank the receptionist and ask for a good date to call and follow up on application reviews. If yes, then wait for your interview, all day if you must. You can prepare by studying the job description.

4. Interview. Whether you obtained your interview by waiting, checking on your application status, or receiving the hiring officer's call, now you are there. (See Chapter Five for more detailed information on interviewing.) The next step is to state your desire for the job at the interview's conclusion. If you receive a job offer, then you have achieved your objective! If you receive a polite no or a "I have a few more candidates to interview," response, thank the interviewer and ask for a good date to follow up on hiring decisions.

5. Follow-up. Send a short thank-you letter to the interviewer, listing two or three positive results of the interview. If the hiring officer provided a date to call, then call on that date. If he provided no date, then call after one week. If the employer has made no decision, let the receptionist or hiring officer advise you of when to call back. You do not want to annoy them, yet you want to communicate your interest. Do not be concerned if the hiring decision takes months. Keep looking!

If you follow the *One More Step* method contacting employers, you will be at the front of the line in vying for the job vacancy. There is such a thing as acting too eager, but it is just as bad to be too hesitant. By displaying confidence without bravura or desperation, you will be poised to meet the interviewer on even terms, negotiate your niche, and create a relationship.

This chapter presents the general résumé, cover letter, reference submission, and application issues, as well as examples taken from different career stages. The rule behind these procedures is to follow the employer's policies at each step.

The Résumé

The résumé is a simple one- or two-page document summarizing your qualifications for the job target. Do not confuse it with a *vita*, which is a comprehensive annotation of accomplishments, experience, and education. You design your résumé to grab the attention of the hiring officer, not to dazzle him with your creativity. There are a few expected formats outlined below.

If you are starting from scratch, first compile your *vita*. See Appendix E for a *vita* worksheet. List everything since high school; if you are a recent graduate, list accomplishments made while young as well. This approach can be an arduous task, but it can be broken down into more manageable increments. Regarding education, you can request your transcripts to get a comprehensive listing with precise dates and grades. For your work experience, call all former employers to verify employment dates, title, salary, location, supervisor, duties, and reason for leaving. Do not omit any civic activities, affiliations, hobbies, or volunteer experience from your worksheet. This is much the same information as requested on a job application, which is presented later in this chapter.

Once you assemble your chronological *vita*, glean from it the details relevant to your job target. Consider having several basic résumés for different occupations at this stage. Remember, the best résumés are not written; they evolve from specific job descriptions. The following are rules for writing a résumé:

- No typographical errors or smudges
- Use a consistent outline style
- Use active voice sentences
- Place your most impressive information at the top and left side
- Structure the document to draw attention to points you want to emphasize by using bullets, boldface type, paragraph indents, or special headings
- Use white, buff, or light grey 20-pound paper with matching blank paper and envelopes for additional correspondence

- Use only black ink
- Different size fonts are acceptable, but make sure the type is clear and faxable
- Staples must be at a 45-degree angle at the top left corner
- If using business-size envelopes, fold correspondence into equal thirds; otherwise, mail documents flat

In addition, this is the secret to the most effective résumé: Tailor your skills to fit the company's job description, classified ad, or concerns expressed over the telephone. You will not be misrepresenting yourself; however, this is your chance to speak their language. Notice also how they have ranked the job requirements in ads or conversation, and list your skills and qualifications in a similar order.

There are different strategies for sending résumés for specific job openings versus a résumé that is to be kept on file. Tailor each résumé and cover letter to fit each job opening. In addition, have a general résumé (with individualized letter) to send to companies for future job openings. With the arrival of word processing, there is no excuse for photocopied materials. Even if you must pay extra, find someone who will keep your job search materials on disc and will expediently print out correct, individualized copies.

It may be worth your while to investigate the benefits of the several résumé software packages on the market. *The Better Working Résumé Kit* has options for different occupational groups. *The Individual Résumé Maker* is recommended for experienced workers with longer employment histories.

Your current employer may help you in writing your résumé; you may take phrases from your job description to aid in summarizing your current position. Also, if you cannot put together your job duties for former jobs, look in the classified ads; many will include relevant job statements that are standard across occupations. Try to use words familiar to your field or profession, those that personnel or hiring officers also will understand, if they have no technical experience.

The following list includes several résumé mistakes to avoid:

- No birthday, photograph, marriage, health, nationality, hobby, membership, salary, or other personal information, unless it directly relates to the job requirements
- Avoid using personal pronouns
- Do not include your present work number unless your boss knows you are looking for another job
- If you have a college degree, omit high school

- If you have no high school degree or GED, leave out education altogether (list on-the-job training under experience)
- If you omit dates, job titles, company names, or locations, interviewers usually assume you are hiding something
- Do not emphasize the negative

There may be problems in your work history you would like to cover up. "Job hopping," or frequent employment turnover, may be diminished by citing the years worked instead of months and years (e.g., 1988, 1989) instead of 3-10/88, 1-4/89. Also, some employers may be eliminated altogether if employment there lasted less than four months or so. The difficulty lies in then completing a company's application, which will likely state something like ". . . any omission, falsification, or incorrect addition of information will result in forfeit of employment status." In other words, if they find anything incorrect, unwittingly or otherwise, they can legally fire or refuse to hire you. Likewise, if your résumé and application do not match, the interviewer may question your credibility.

How to handle other difficult questions about your employment background will be discussed in the next chapter on Interviewing. However, you can use additional strategies on your résumé. Applicants of advanced age can limit their work histories to the past seven to ten years, while listing additional job titles together in a one-paragraph summary. As mentioned before, lack of a high school diploma can be hidden by eliminating the EDUCATION heading and listing relevant training or transferable skills under EXPERIENCE. Similarly, if you seek a career change and your experience is clearly from a different background, develop a separate heading that lists your skills transferring into the new career.

It is perfectly acceptable to list relevant volunteer experience or hobbies if they directly relate to your job target or career change. It also can demonstrate your ability to organize, motivate, and work with others. Many Washingtonians parlay journalism internships, political activist volunteer experience, or writing hobbies into paid positions. In some competitive fields, it may be the only way to break in.

Most Washington employers view military experience positively. If you have more than a short service record, have a separate heading for MILITARY or SERVICE. Otherwise, list it under EXPERIENCE (or however you choose to label your work) if it has been within the last seven to ten years. Again, if your military career does not relate to your job target, it may be best to minimize it in your résumé.

Additional information, such as career objective, salary, desired location or shift, right to work in the United States, or transportation issues, are best left to be discussed in the cover letter. Do not address these issues, however, unless the employer requests it explicitly. Always use the same job title the employer uses and check to see whether personnel assigns numbers to the vacancies.

The following are examples of résumés at different career stages: entry-level, mid-career, and management/corporate. Cover letters and a reference sheets follow the résumés. A résumé should never be submitted without a cover letter.

ENTRY-LEVEL RÉSUMÉ

Will E. Makitt
1666 Yellow Brick Road; Falls Church, VA 20246; (703) 555-1666

EDUCATION

BS Computer Science—Former Statesman University, Fairfax, VA, 5/90. Minor in Math and Applied Statistics. GPA 3.37/4.00 (cum laude), with GPA 3.52/4.00 in major subject, Computer Science.

Related Courses: **FORTRAN**, Numerical Methods (Advanced FORTRAN), **COBOL**, Large Files (Advanced COBOL), Data Structures (**PL/6**), Assembler Language (**Intel 8080**), Modern Programming Languages (**C, Ada, COBOL 8x, LOGO, Pascal**), and Data Base (IDS II). Also used IBM RS-6000 and Data General.

EXPERIENCE

Programmer Intern—Exploding Star Electronics Corporation, Falls Church, VA, 1-8/89. Worked in the Scientific Computer Services Department, providing support to Exploding Star headquarters. Maintained existing programs, created and debugged system of programs for personnel files, and participated in analysis of several major projects. Used C/UNIX on an IBM RS-6000 and Exploding Star personal computers.

Crew Trainer—Archibald's Restaurant, Fairfax, VA, summers/86-88. Trained new employees; promoted from cook and cashier.

HONORS AND ACHIEVEMENTS

Distinguished Achievers' Scholarship—FSU, 1986-90.

Member—Data Processing Management Association, 1989-present.

Member—Alpha Phi Omega National Service Fraternity, 1987-90. Treasurer, 1989-90.

REFERENCES

Available from Career Development Center, FSU, 4400 University Drive, Fairfax, VA 22030; (703) 555-2601.

MID-CAREER-LEVEL RÉSUMÉ

BILL D. WALLS
4215 Cinder Block Street
Rockville, MD 20851
(301) 555-4215

OBJECTIVE:

To secure a management position implementing my knowledge of the cement finishing and construction industry.

EXPERIENCE:

1985-91   Foreman—Structurect, Rockville, MD. Promoted from Cement Finisher.

1984-85   Cement Finisher—London Bridge Companies, Silver Spring, MD.

1960-84   Lead Man—Sides Contractors, Little Rock, AR, relocated to Rockville, MD.

SKILLS:

Supervising—hiring and firing; training; monitoring; completing log for personnel, equipment, and supplies; ordering inventory; scheduling; and working as a liaison between superintendent and laborers.

Cement Mason—curbs, gutters, sidewalks, driveways, steps, porches, walls, basements; includes light carpentry, surveying, and reading blueprints.

Operating Machinery—backhoes, dozers, loaders, power tools, and "Cleveland 92 Trencher."

Computers—WordPerfect and Lotus; reading ADP sheets.

EDUCATION:

1957   GED—US Marine Corps, Twentynine Palms, CA.

References provided on request.

MANAGEMENT/CORPORATE LEVEL RÉSUMÉ

RICH D. ZIRE, CPC   100-K Bank Alley
(202) 555-1001   Washington, DC 20007

EDUCATION Professional: Certified Pension Consultant (CPC) obtained from The American Society of Pension Actuaries, 5/89. Three of ten courses completed toward the Certified Employee Benefits Specialist (CEBS) through the Whig School of The University of New England.

College: Wahoo University, Charlottesville, VA. Bachelor's Degree in Business, 5/82. Currently enrolled at Turtle University, College Park, MD, College of Business and Management's MBA Program.

EXPERIENCE

Suspendadollar Pension Services—Silver Spring, MD, 10/86 to present. Promoted from Financial Services.
Responsibilities include:
- Marketing investment products and administrative services
- Supporting the distribution system
- Designing, enrolling, and servicing all types of qualified retirement plans
- Conducting educational seminars
Achievements:
- Played integral role in the Mid-Atlantic region topping company's revenue goals for several years
- Attained two company trip awards

Suspendadollar Financial Services, Rockville, MD, 6/85-10/86.
Responsibilities included:
- Marketing consumer mortgage loans
- Performing credit and budget analyses
- Evaluating real estate and other collateral
- Controlling the profit margin of a branch office
Achievements:
- Promoted to Branch Manager in eleven months
- Led the district in loan production prior to promotion

An American Insurance Company, Richmond, VA, 1/83-5/85. This national company has 3000 agents and 250 branches.
Responsibilities included:
- Marketing life insurance and annuity products
- Training new personnel
Achievements:
- Named company's 14th most productive agent
- Promoted to Assistant Manager of 3rd most productive office

SKILLS   WordPerfect 5.1, Lotus 1-2-3, and dBase IV.

REFERENCES   Request references sheet.

The Cover Letter and References Sheet

The cover letter is your chance to demonstrate your communication skills. This is the first sample of your work. Because all jobs require some sort of record-keeping or report writing, the cover letter should be good. Follow all rules of business letters: Allow no typos or smudges, use the same stationery and fonts as in your résumé, keep the length to one page, and heed the employer's specific requests. Use direct, active voice sentences with good grammar. Do not try to be humorous.

Pay attention to this note about a potential mistake: DO NOT PRINT COVER LETTERS ON YOUR CURRENT EMPLOYER'S LETTERHEAD. Not only is this against etiquette, but also it sends a powerful message to employers about your lack of trustworthiness. Also, a cover letter must never be handwritten in Washington, even for a blue collar job.

You also could commit job-searching suicide by sending a photocopied general cover letter to employers. Such a letter shows a lack of commitment and interest in fitting in with the company. It is the equivalent of sending a xeroxed letter to every personal ad in the *Washingtonian*, and expecting to get a date. What might happen? You could get a response from only the desperate. You would likely not enjoy working there.

The beginning of the cover letter should be addressed formally. Unless the company has specifically requested no telephone calls, call the Employment Coordinator or Hiring Officer to get the job description, confirm the officer's name (and gender), and the employer's mailing address. At this time, you may also determine whether they are accepting résumés in person or by fax. In any case, you will need a cover letter. Under the salutation, state that the letter is being sent regarding (RE:) and then state the exact job title. If you are responding to a "blind" ad to a post office box, address the letter to Employment Coordinator or Hiring Officer. If the ad lists the company without a telephone number, look it up, even if you have to read a whole section to determine what the company's acronym represents.

The first paragraph of your cover letter should tell how you found the vacancy. If your letter accompanies a résumé to be kept for future openings, tell how you identified the company as a desirable place to work. In other words, begin the process of creating the relationship by emphasizing how you will fit in with the employer. Also, you can get their attention with a strong statement about why you want to work there, but be careful not to sound overbearing. Consider how outgoing you must be for your job target. Present yourself accordingly, and you will feel more comfortable with the letter as well.

The second paragraph of your cover letter should establish how your skills fit in with the employer's job requirements. Stick to qualifications relevant to the job and state them in measurable qualities, if possible (i.e., type 65 words per minute, supervised 15 employees, established and worked within $250,000 budget, etc.). If you had the opportunity to talk to the hiring officer, cite some reasons identified during the discussion concerning his agreement to accept your résumé. This section can be two paragraphs if necessary.

The last paragraph of your cover letter should confirm your desire to interview and learn more as well as provide any salary requirements or other requested information. You may confirm a scheduled interview or state your schedule availability. The closing sentence should be a positive, hopeful request for future contact or correspondence.

Make sure to include any additional documents requested, such as references, transcripts, writing samples, driving record, application, or other forms. In these cases, be sure to note "enclosures" at the end of the cover letter. It is also a good idea to prepare a references sheet. Some employers ask for it simultaneously with the résumé; others wait until the application or the interview. Do not provide your references until requested, even if they are impeccable. You want employers to form an opinion about you firsthand.

Regarding references, call each person before providing his name to an employer. First, you need to ask permission. Second, you need to determine whether he feels comfortable giving you a positive report. You can then obtain his correctly spelled name, address, and telephone number. You also can use this opportunity to begin networking. It is a good idea to send your references a thank-you letter and include your résumé so they can discuss your qualifications intelligently.

Some possible sources for references include teachers, friends in established businesses, former coworkers or employers, or the clergy. Pick anyone who is familiar with your work or character. You should not use your family.

Here are three examples of cover letters designed to accompany the résumés above at entry-level, mid-career, and management/corporate levels. Following will be a sample reference sheet.

ENTRY-LEVEL COVER LETTER

Will E. Makitt
1666 Yellow Brick Road
Falls Church, VA 20246
(703) 555-1666

May 15, 1990

Malcolm Pewter, Manager
Very Important High Tech Company
3000 Jefferson Davis Highway
Suite 700
Arlington, VA 22202

RE: Associate Programmer/Analyst

Dear Mr. Pewter:

Please find enclosed my résumé regarding your *Washington Post* advertisement for an associate programmer/analyst. Having recently graduated from Former Statesman University with a bachelor's degree in computer science, I am ready to begin my professional career.

During my senior year and internship at Exploding Star, I specialized in UNIX/C programming, which I noted was your primary qualification. I used these programs to construct, analyze, and debug a system for the Personnel Department, for tracking employees' use of health insurance and sick leave. I also participated in management group analysis of several ongoing projects, which included the accessibility of the accounts payable and receivable systems, the customer service system, and production quality control.

I am eager to learn of the support you provide to your users and clients. I am available to interview immediately and at your convenience. I hope to hear from you soon.

Sincerely,

Will E. Makitt

Will E. Makitt

WEM
enclosure

MID-CAREER-LEVEL COVER LETTER

BILL D. WALLS
4215 Cinder Block Street
Rockville, MD 20851
(301) 555-4215

March 27, 1992

Frank N. Stone, Superintendent
Stone's Masonry
911 Quarry Road
Gaithersburg, MD 20878

RE: Construction Foreman

Dear Mr. Stone:

Regarding the above position, please examine my qualifications as listed on the enclosed résumé. I have over 30 years experience in the cement finishing industry and have supervised laborers for much of that time.

As we discussed, if I were to work for Stone's Masonry, I would like to accomplish a 15-25 percent growth during my first year. I also believe my contacts in the construction business would contribute to increased subcontracting. I can motivate men to deliver optimum productivity with a minimum of turnover. I am confident I can learn your record system for personnel, supplies, and equipment management.

I look forward to meeting you at my 11:00 a.m. April 2 inteview. At this time, I will bring my project portfolio and references. Please call if there are any details you wish to discuss.

Sincerely,

Bill D. Walls

Bill D. Walls

BDW
enclosure

MANAGEMENT/CORPORATE LEVEL COVER LETTER

RICH D. ZIRE, CPC
100-K Bank Alley
Washington, DC 20007
(202) 555-1001

June 23, 1992

Hiring Officer
Washington Post Employment
Box M-XXXX
1150 15th Street, NW
Washington, DC 20071

RE: Retirement Portfolio Manager

Dear Officer:

I submit my résumé for your consideration. As I understand from your *Washington Post* advertisement, you seek a financial professional to manage your marketing and service staff. I have the direct financial service and management experience you seek, and the expertise to lead others to excellence.

I am eager to learn of your company's structure. As you can see, my experience is based on the insurance industry, which I have complemented with my MBA study. I will graduate in December, 1992. I know cash management, investments, trust services, annuities, and commercial lending policies and practices. I have a solid history of getting results and motivating others.

You did not mention what software packages you utilize; I currently work with Lotus 1-2-3, dBase IV, and WordPerfect 5.1. I have devised employee tests for these systems as well to assess my effectiveness in training my support staff. I am confident I will quickly learn your systems.

Please contact me soon for an interview. I will commute throughout the Washington Metropolitan area. As you requested, my salary requirements are a base salary of $40,000. I hope to learn more about the job and your company soon.

Sincerely,

Rich D. Zire

Rich D. Zire, CPC

RDZ
Enclosure

REFERENCES SHEET

RICH D. ZIRE, CPC 100-K Bank Alley
(202) 555-1001 Washington, DC 20007

PROFESSIONAL REFERENCES

Lucretia Cash, Vice President
Money Grubbing Holding and Trust
7999 Sidewinder Avenue
Richmond, VA 23214
(804) 555-7999 (w)
(804) 555-4637 (h)

Victor N. Venture
Simultaneous Mutual Benefits
2099 K Street, NW
Suite 1900
Washington, DC 20036
(202) 555-1900 (w)
(202) 555-5646 (h)

Jeannie S. Power, CEO
The Very Smart Investment Company
325 Deluxe Court
McLean, VA 22101
(703) 555-0325 (w)
(703) 555-0326 (h)

PERSONAL REFERENCES

Randy Fleet
540 Seamen's Wharf
Norfolk, VA 23503
(804) 555-5442 (h)

Tony Raiment
1993 Saint Laurent Drive
Chevy Chase, MD 20815
(301) 555-8965 (h)

Row D. Brothers
889 Fraternity Circle
University Park, MD 20782
(301) 555-5549 (h)

Sending the Documents

When mailing letters, consider overnight mail, but do not hinge your hopes on this technique. Secretaries and receptionists often open the mail and then automatically discard the big, colorful, overnight mail packets. If, on the other hand, you must submit correspondence before a deadline, this is a useful option.

When faxing any document, always follow it up with a hard copy (original) through the mail. If an employer prefers not to receive résumés by fax, then overnight mail or hand delivery is nearly as fast and appears more professional.

Hand delivery of a résumé may appear too eager for a management/corporate level applicant. This technique is irreplaceable for observing the work place, but not at the cost of losing an interview. If you feel comfortable, proceed to deliver in person, but be polite and brief. At the corporate level, do not ask for an interview, and you will likely not be required to complete an application.

The Application

So, you have written your résumé, cover letter, and references sheet; have verified the information; and learned how to adapt them for different jobs and employers. You are now ready to visit the employer and complete the application. As mentioned before, dress ready to interview (see the next chapter).

Prepare yourself with a completed sample application (see below) and extra copies of your résumé and references sheet. Also bring copies of documents authorizing your right to work in the United States; such documents may include a passport, certificate of US citizenship, certificate of naturalization, a driver's license or US military card, together with a Social Security card, birth certificate, or employment authorization (green card). Any additional documents specific to your profession (license, driving record, writing samples, design portfolio, etc.) should be included.

While in the employer's office, you have an excellent chance to observe the atmosphere, the workers, and any of your competitors who may be there as well. See if the office is well-kept and furnished, and if the people there seem pleasant. You want to find a company that is financially and emotionally healthy, and dilapidated desks or tense employees do not bode well. If possible, make small talk with the receptionist to see if the turnover rate is high and what possible causes might be. You may also want to learn why the position you seek is vacant. Also, watch others applying for the job to see how you compare in terms of professional or appropriate appearance. If they have typed their applications or brought portfolios, make sure you have prepared as well.

Applications are different from résumés as they document more complete information, and employers have more control over them. They generally ask about an applicant's whole name, address, telephone, authorization to work in the United States, job title sought, salary desired, all schools attended, graduation results, other training, licensing, technical skills, previous employment with the company, criminal record, military service, physical ability to perform the job, whether you have been fired or laid off, references, and employment history for the previous ten years.

Under employment history, they will ask company name, address, telephone, position title, employment dates (month and year), salary, supervisor, department, duties, and reason for leaving. Take pains to ensure that this information is true and complete. Never simply put, "See résumé." To help you collect this information, see Appendix E for a *vita* worksheet. You can then determine what information you need to check or obtain.

One thing you must remember when calling schools and former employers to verify the above information: If they cannot trace it for you, they probably will not trace it for prospective employers. This allows some leverage in preparing your job search packet.

Since most employers ask for the same information, an easy way to complete an application is to prepare these answers before visiting the employer. Carry them in your job search notebook together with copies of any other documents the employer requires. You also can formulate responses to sensitive questions, such as reasons for leaving, periods of unemployment, lack of professional licensing, criminal conviction, or physical handicap.

State these answers to sensitive questions in a positive way, emphasizing your current ability and desire to work (e.g., "I did not agree with management's policies, but they are out of business now, and I am eager to present my ideas to you"). It is a rare interviewer, even in Washington, who will not dismiss one employment transgression if everything else is acceptable. Yet, an undesirable history or pattern will likely prevent you from even gaining an interview. If this is the case, your best strategy is to continue working where you are

to establish stability. If you are unemployed, aim below your qualifications to be more competitive.

Answer every question on the application, even if it is to note
N/A, meaning not applicable to your situation. Use a black pen to
neatly print all answers. Employers will view your completed application as another sample of your work, just like the cover letter.
Supervisors attend to how neatly, completely, and concisely you express yourself. To them, it indicates how you well you will work, even
if your job is not completing applications all day.

Be aware if you complete the application in person, the secretary
or hiring officer may watch to see how long it takes you to finish.
They also will wait to see whether you came prepared, and especially
if you brought someone to help you write. If you really cannot complete it independently, ask to take the application with you, which
you will return completed. Typing the application does not hurt.
However, many employers do not release the application form outside
their offices.

There are some questions employers may ask that could be illegal,
depending on how they ask them. Laws vary with jurisdictions, but
generally such illegal questions are similar to the information you
should not provide on your résumé: age (if older than 18 and younger
than 65), photograph, marriage, health, race, nationality, religion,
hobby, social membership or affiliation, or arrest status. Again, if
employers phrase questions relating the issues directly to your ability
to do the job, they may not be illegal. Still, if they ask sensitive
questions and you decline to answer, they may perceive you as difficult. If you really want to work there, answer the questions anyway.
If you get a bad feeling about their invasion of your privacy, ask about
this in the interview.

The SF-171

We have touched on other difficulties in the job-search, but certainly
the federal government's job application, Standard Form-171, at four
(sometimes more) pages, seems overwhelming to complete. There
are many business services in this town that complete SF-171s or
give you specific advice on how to complete them yourself. You must
remember personnel offices look at each SF-171 as more work to do.
The following hints can help you to make sure yours gets processed:

• Put the job title and vacancy announcement number on each
  application.

- Apply by the closing date.
- Include all required forms, and only those forms.
- Sign and date each application in black ink.
- Request a vacancy announcement before submitting the SF-171 to ensure that your qualifications meet the requirements.

There is a software package that assists in completing the SF-171, called *Quick and Easy for the SF-171*. If you have a laser printer, it will recreate the entire form with your information. Other printers must use a blank form. *Quick and Easy* is a helpful program, but you must know enough about the vacancy announcement to shape the responses purposefully. The program is available in versions for only one or two applicants, but it can save hundreds of variations under the applicant's Social Security number.

If you must complete your SF-171 independently and without a computer program, type an original with all the information which never changes: name, address, birthday, etc. Most people photocopy the applications, leaving blank the date and the job announcement title and number, then filling in that information for each application. An original green application is a nice touch, and communicates your undivided ambition for that job.

Next, just as you make your résumé job specific, organize your qualifications to those on the vacancy announcement. Similarly, state them in specific, measurable terms (e. g., organized the numerical filing system and maintained an alphabetized cross-reference file, supervised three helpers, etc.). Try to document a consistent career path throughout your work history. You may be competing with someone for whom the vacancy was created, and the announcement was worded to fit his qualifications as well. Be positive and tenacious when seeking a government position.

Summary

The following points summarize the process of contacting the employer under the criteria of an ideal scenario:

1. Hear about the vacancy from your best friend on Sunday.
2. Call the hiring officer to get a sense of the job description Monday morning.
3. Deliver your tailored résumé and cover letter Monday afternoon, observe the office, get a company pamphlet, and schmooze with the receptionist.

4. Receive a call from the hiring officer Tuesday, scheduling an interview for Wednesday.
5. Arrive 45 minutes early Wednesday to complete the application.
6. Interview for 90 minutes and leave your references sheet.
7. Fax a thank-you note on Thursday.
8. Receive a call on Friday with your job offer.

Sometimes it is that easy. Most of the time, Beltway traffic, your current job, your competition, and temperamental technology get in the way. With persistence and a little luck, you will prevail.

By now you must think the job search process is impossible because of the relentless research and surveillance required of your potential employers. Information gained from these efforts cannot be replaced by hearsay. You must find out for yourself. Allow for this investment in time to prevent later unnecessary applications and interviews. You will also avert accepting a job offer before learning of an employer's high turnover rate or fraudulent business practices. With persistence, you will find the employers you want, gain interviews, and receive trustworthy job offers.

Chapter Five

INTERVIEWING

If you have made it this far, relax a little. Most of the hard work is over. Every Psych 101 teaching assistant will tell you "moderate arousal" will get you your best test performance. An interview is a test, not just of expertise, but of how you present yourself personally. If you have done your homework and know something about the employer, you should seek to interview the hiring officer as well.

When seeking to fit in with an employer, both sides should feel comfortable with factors such as culture, education, gender, politics, appearance, health, age, or even financial status. We can all expound on the evils of prejudice, but when it comes to allowing strangers into their workplace, employers usually pick those who are most like themselves. Similarly, applicants look to the employer to be like a second family. It may not be right or intelligent, but it is the standard.

Do not let this finding overwhelm you. While some liken pleasing the interviewer to trying to understand the opposite gender, it does not have to be an impossible or dreaded event. If you approach a job for which you qualify, have done your research, and want to rise above your competitors, you have several interview options: Be your polite self and take your chances they will like you; mainstream your behavior, which hopefully will be attractive to them and within your tolerance; or try to copy their style, appearance, rhythm, and language, and if they like themselves they will like you.

You have to decide what is best for your situation, but remember that interviewing is a two-way street. Generally, if jobs are few, you must try harder to fit in. If jobs are plentiful in your field, you can be choosy and look for an employer like yourself. If the employer has granted you an interview, then be confident you have done everything correctly so far. Hiring officers do not spend time interviewing people when they have no interest. Take this confidence into the meeting.

When you receive a call for an interview, be ready to work out a mutually convenient date, time, and place, and confirm the interviewer's name and title. Allow about two hours for the interview; most last around 30 minutes. They may administer short intelligence or aptitude screening tests as well, although this is the exception rather than the rule. Additionally, employers will let you know up front about any physical examination or drug screening requirements.

This chapter will outline the interview steps: how to prepare, first impression, first half (presentation of company and job), second half (questions from and to the interviewer), closing, and follow-up options. Remember the emphasis is to create and develop the employment relationship during the interview. Show them how you can fit in.

Preparation

While you complete their application, gather information about the company. What is its business? If it is a government office, what is its mission? How long have they been in existence? What do they see as their economic (or service) forecast for growth? Do not be shy about asking for a pamphlet on the agency or business from the receptionist; be careful, however, of asking for too much (e.g., marketing portfolios, financial statements, or employee statistics). If you should try this, businesses will think you are from a competitor and the government will think you are a spy.

Instead, try other means of evaluating the employer. Call the local Chamber of Commerce to see about their business ratings. The chamber's staff may also be familiar with the employer's reputation. If you know someone who works there, you are in a position to get the inside information you really want to know. The public library is also a great source for directories and newspapers with business ratings. Consult the reference librarian. Do not rely completely on any one of these methods but use them in assembling a comprehensive picture of the employer. Study the information you gain for asking questions during the second half of your interview (see below).

As discussed in the previous chapter, you should attempt to visit the employer to deliver your résumé or complete an application to observe the work atmosphere. Dress ready to interview, that is, as you would expect your supervisor to dress everyday. Then, if you visit in person, you can verify how your interviewer or prospective boss really looks. This is the secret discovered by John Milloy, author of *Dress for Success*. His research indicated fashion trends will come and go, but the appearance of fitting in with the boss can be a dependable factor in getting the job.

Milloy's message is that you can over- or under-dress for the interview. If the interviewer wears a Wall Street uniform, copy it. Such an image means conservative hairstyle, tan overcoat, navy blue suit, white shirt, red tie, and conservative shoes for the men. For the ladies, the image includes two-inch pumps, closed heel and toe. If the boss wears jeans, a flannel shirt, and cowboy boots, try to wear a serious version of this outfit. The point is, know the style of the work place before the interview, while showing your seriousness about the job. To help you define the style, examine the mode of dress for these variables: conservative or contemporary, frugal or expensive, formal or casual, and drab or colorful.

If you really cannot survey the workplace before the interview, then visit a competitor, although this may not be completely accurate (consider applying there as well). You will likely know enough about your field to guess what to wear but, when in doubt, be conservative. Use the following checklist for a conservative interview appearance:

- Be sure you have a conservative hairstyle and no facial hair.
- Use a moderate amount of makeup and jewelry for women, none for men.
- Use extra antiperspirant and no noticeable cologne.
- Arrive with no holes in socks or stockings; women carry an extra pair.
- Check that there are no stains, hanging threads, or wrinkles in clothing.
- Be sure that shoes are polished and clean.
- Wear a well-fitting suit for a professional position.
- Wear work clothing for a blue-collar position.

In addition, consider that an employer might observe you in the parking lot outside the building. Run your car through the carwash and clean out the trash. If it has obvious appearance flaws, borrow a car if possible. Do not bring anyone to the interview with you.

In keeping with the conservative theme, glasses can give you a more intellectual appearance. Carry your job search materials in a briefcase or portfolio that coordinates with your outfit, especially with your shoes. Above everything else in this book, follow the observed style of the boss and employees.

First Impression

Some interviewers say the first six seconds are the interview, and all the rest is fluff. In any event, practice until perfect getting your simultaneous greeting right:

1. Eye contact.
2. Smile.
3. Handshake; firm, warm, and dry.
4. Confident introduction of self.

Arrive 45 minutes early if you need to complete an application or 15 minutes early just to wait. You should verify this prior to arriving. Use the wait time to keep hands warm and dry. If they offer you a beverage, it is all right to accept it. Just make sure you do not spill it under any circumstances. When you see the interviewer, call him by name greet him warmly. Let the employer define the next part. He will usually lead the way to the room and offer you a seat. Mind your manners.

Show enthusiasm for the position! Just as you did in your cover letter, show yourself to be the type of person who will work in the job; but turn up the volume a little just to sell yourself. Do not be too timid to ask for what you want, but at the same time do not impinge on anyone else to get it. Be confident, but not obnoxious.

First Half

Interviewers usually reserve the first half of the session for defining the company and the job opening. Let the interviewer talk and give him your full attention. Do not take notes, although you may feel you should. Make mental notes of two or three details to ask about later.

Try to sit beside the interviewer if possible. Otherwise, face the interviewer and lean slightly forward occasionally. Do not touch him after the handshake. Even if the job is a massage therapist, wait until you have established a relationship with the interviewer (i.e., received a job offer) to invade personal space. For other body language, have shoulders relaxed, hands in lap, legs crossed under the chair, and briefcase (or job search materials) at your side. Do not chew gum, smoke, pick your nails, look at your watch, or otherwise make annoying or nervous behaviors. Practice this. But again, observe the interviewer's style and behave similarly.

Protocol is even more significant if a small business owner interviews you, and he will make the hiring decision. This individual will definitely want someone who will fit in with himself and other employees. For instance, if he smokes three cigarettes during the interview, and you happen to be a smoker, go ahead and smoke one cigarette. Be slightly more conservative than the interviewer.

When applying to large companies, the interviewer will likely have the power to eliminate candidates, rather than the authority to hire. It will be somewhat difficult to see what people dress or act like there, so trust your instincts about your profession. Also, you can expect much higher scrutiny from interviewers as a higher corporate level. Conservative and mainstream are dependable principles to observe.

Do not let an interviewer offend you by not following format, knowing your résumé thoroughly, or otherwise worshiping the ground you walk on. Some employers will throw "curve balls;" for instance, they may surprise you with a panel of interviewers (give them all fresh copies of your résumé), take you out to dinner to watch your table manners (demonstrate manners slightly better than theirs), try to see how intoxication influences your behavior (drink less than they do), or try to pick a fight. Recognize these techniques for what they are: that is, more questions on their test for employment. They want to examine your substance. Regarding the fight, you must decide whether aggressiveness is integral to the job. If it is, show them you can hold your ground.

Some interviewers will ask leading questions to trick you into admitting some sort of fault or transgression, by alluding that such a failing is acceptable or even desirable. In your quest to fit in, you could inadvertently condone inappropriate business practices or worse. Do not let common sense escape your quest for the perfect interview. Use your judgement in discerning the employer and stop if you feel manipulated or uncomfortable.

Many interviewers like to do most of the talking, while they carefully watch your reactions. Let the interviewer set the tone. Still, if you get one who seems reluctant to talk, then ask him questions to get the expected information. You can then take control and talk about how you relate to the company's objectives. If you do not have much experience with interviews, just remember to define your skills as relevant to the job.

The first half of the interview is an excellent time to show off your knowledge of the company by making a few complimentary statements about their services or products. Do not overdo this; follow the interviewer's lead. Center your concentration on the interview. A boring interviewer does not a bad company make, but a dozing one perhaps. This is your opportunity to learn about where you could be spending your waking hours. Prepare to find out all that you can.

Second Half—Answering Questions

The second half of the session is the time for questions and answers. After the interviewer has framed the company and the job, he will likely ask for information from you. Many interviewers will ask seemingly impertinent questions; they neither have time to be polite nor ask about superficial details. They must get to know you quickly and perhaps find your flaws. Still, most are reasonable. If you keep in mind you must define your qualifications to fit in with the company, you will do well.

Prepare at this time for technical questions related to your field. One strategy is to beat the interviewer to the punch by asking questions about the job and then relating your qualifications to it.

The difficulty comes when they ask you a question, and you do not know the company's policy about it. Since your goal is fitting in, be honest, but state your answer or expectations in reasonable and positive terms. Focus on the task at hand—your employment—and do not let the interviewer deviate unless the job is directly relevant to another subject.

Memorize examples of your career objectives, flexibility, trainability, formal education, compatibility with coworkers, problem-solving, quantity of work, quality of work, attendance, punctuality, and preferred management style. Just as you did with your résumé, state these objectives in active voice sentences in measurable and quantifiable terms. Here are some examples:

"I identified and serviced 34 new contracts in two years with no attrition."

"I am never late. I like to arrive 30 minutes early to have a cup of coffee and organize my work for the day."

"I think I used three sick days last year, which is normal for me."

"I like to work with a team. In school, I found others seeking my direction for projects. Since starting work, I have been a resource person in my office as well."

"Oh yes, when all the phones went out, it just unnerved me. So I caught up on letter and report writing and put away a stack of closed files."

"I generally prefer a supervisor who will meet with me every day or two at first and then turn me loose after about a month."

"Realistically, I would like to move into a management position within five years. I expect to start my MBA next year and identified your company for the tuition reimbursement and manager training programs."

Be sure to speak in a clear voice, and look at the interviewer when talking. Also, it is usually best to try to mainstream any noticeable dialect. This is not a steadfast rule; keep the job in mind. To whom will you be communicating verbally and how much? Any telephone jobs will go to people who can speak clearly. Sometimes a specific, understandable, foreign dialect is an asset, such as a high-end sales or public relations position.

One famous interview question is, "What is your greatest weakness?" We have all been told to reply, "Modesty." If your reference point is to create a relationship, and you want to feel as comfortable with a company as possible, then admit to two or three. If you have trouble getting to work by 8:00 a.m., some may not view that as a major hindrance, but others might. If you find you work best when left alone, an interviewer may state that this is right in line with company objectives.

If the competition is strong and you really want the job, frame one fault in a positive way. For example, you might say, "I'm a perfectionist on my reports, so sometimes I don't have them ready by the due date, but I have improved since learning word processing." If you want to test the company to see how reasonable they are, ask them directly about their policies. Be honest about where you think you might experience difficulty.

Never speak negatively about a previous employer, even if they deserve it. Never answer questions with a simple yes or no; explain further, but not at the length of a dissertation. And what about humor? If you can manage to communicate seriousness about the job, a little humor might round out your interview. Let the interviewer lead the way.

There are some other questions often asked during an interview. It is a good idea to think these issues through before the interview.

Practicing answers aloud or participating in a mock interview will further hone your presentation skills. Consider these:
- Tell me about yourself.
- Tell me why you want the job.
- What can you contribute to our company?
- Why did you choose your profession?
- What do you like about working?
- How did previous employers treat you?
- What do you consider your greatest mistake in college?
- What types of people offend you?
- How do you handle deadlines?
- Are you willing to relocate?
- Do you have any personal obligations that would detract from work?
- Tell me about your favorite job.
- How do you resolve personal confrontations?

If the interviewer has done his homework, he will pick out any blemish on your otherwise perfect record. He will confront you about the "D" in Quantum Literature or the eight-month lapse in employment between your work as a life-guard and a tax consultant. He may ask about that time you were fired because you were the only one to wear a Halloween costume to work or your period of medical recovery after the tragic electrolysis accident.

Whatever your personal taboo, one every five years or so is acceptable, depending on the job's level of responsibility. Take the initiative. Tell the truth (in a positive light), stress your commitment to working, and perhaps ask the interviewer how crucial it is to have untested employees. Because of your experience, you can put work into perspective, appreciate it, and give it your complete and serious attention.

Major gaps between jobs can be explained by listing specific accomplishments during those periods. Do not be afraid to state the truth but frame it in a positive way. Recovery from a long illness or injury is acceptable; emphasize your renewed health and willingness to work. Taking time out for family issues, such as raising children or caring for parents, is also common. However, the employer will be concerned that these issues will continue to take time and energy away from work. You must be prepared to state your commitment to the job, if only during working hours. If nothing else, you can cite home improvement or travel as accomplishments during any periods of lay-off or lack of work.

On the other hand, if your record clearly shows a recurring problem, you must think about what you can do to intervene. No amount of explaining will wipe out a penchant for fighting, gambling, sleeping late, or other causes of missing work. If you have a job, stay with it and seek help. If you need a job, aim low compared to your qualifications but try for one with good health benefits.

Asking Questions

Now it is your turn to ask questions. If things are smooth so far, do not wreck it by being too invasive. Yet, you want to know what the company is like to make an informed decision before commitment. If you have done your homework as well, you may uncover their blemishes. These are questions people commonly wish they had asked during interviews:
- Why is the position open?
- What kind of preparation or training will there be?
- Where and with whom will I be working?
- To whom will my supervisor report?
- What is the career path for this position?
- What kind of training is encouraged for this position?
- What are the company's growth plans?
- What are the company's weaknesses; how can my position help?
- What is the staff turnover rate per year?
- When would you want me to start?

If the interviewer provides you with acceptable answers and does not seem to hide anything, then perhaps you have found a winner. Do not be surprised if the interviewer then throws a completely unexpected or wild card question. It is not over until the employer makes a hiring decision.

The following are signs that the interview is going your way: the interviewer's smiling a great deal, giving you information about choosing health plans, adopting a more casual conversation style, offering you more money than you expected, asking you for other possible candidates to fill positions within the company, or talking disparagingly about other candidates. Let this give you confidence, but do not relax completely.

Stop at this point and decide how badly you want this job. Think about how easy it will be for you to fit in. If you absolutely need the job, then tell the interviewer you want to be hired. If you have prepared pat statements you are sure the employer wants to hear, relax and let him make you an offer. If you are instead seeking a career upgrade, see if you are comfortable with the relationship you have created. You are ready to talk salary.

Do not broach the subject of your salary until the interviewer does. Let him bring up money, benefits, perqs, carpools, intramurals, and other details of the job. If you pay undue attention to these subjects, he will likely think you do not place working as your top priority, even during work hours. If he offers you a job and then stands to escort you to the door, you need to let him know he forgot something.

When you start salary negotiations, consider the strategy of the interviewer. It is extremely intricate to ascertain this before the event, but some will want to haggle over money and benefits, while others will want to make you a definite offer for you to accept or reject. Most will return the responsibility back to you by asking for your salary requirements. Come to an agreement early. Star quarterbacks aside, you do not want to be perceived as difficult.

If you have done your research, you will know what a reasonable salary is and what you may be worth. When an interviewer offers a salary range much lower or higher than you expect, this could indicate that the employer is not desirable. A salary too low may suggest financial problems, while one too high may indicate difficulty retaining staff. Everyone wants a high salary, but you need to question the interviewer about the salary range and the stability of the company.

If you are flexible regarding a lower salary in exchange for other benefits, such as more frequent performance reviews, say so. If things do not progress well in this regard, ask the interviewer what he expects. Both sides must compromise if both are to be satisfied. Forge ahead. This is your chance to discuss what you want. However, agreeing on a reasonable salary does not mean you have the job. At this point, you are ready to close the interview.

Closing

Do not be discouraged if the interview is coming to a close and there has been no salary negotiations. If you want the job at the end of the interview, say so. Many employers will give the job to the candidate whom they feel wants it the most—on the assumption that he will work the hardest and remain with the company. This is not the time to play hard to get.

Watch the interviewer for signs the interview is over. He may straighten his papers, look at his watch, roll his eyes, sigh, or show other signs of boredom. Most interviewers will simply request to finish the meeting. When you get these signals, do not continue talking about how wonderful you are. Get ready for the final five minutes.

If you have some reservations about the employer, this is the time to express them. Maybe you still want to find that dream company where all the employees happily come to work an hour early, just because they have so much fun. At this time, you may want to ask them what they will do to resolve any problems you have discovered. If they plan to allow vacations this year and will put it in writing, for example, that is a positive sign. If the video game and tanning bed room is nearing completion, so much the better. If, however, you know your competition is breathing down your neck in the next waiting room, then you should not come across as so demanding.

If you sense the employer has reservations about you at the end of the interview, this is the time to resolve them. Ask plainly, "What do you see as hindering factors to hiring me for this job?" If the interviewer is honest, then you can address any of his concerns to either correct his perceptions or assure him of your plans to increase/improve your skills. This is the time to show strength and confidence.

Your departure should be similar to your greeting: eye contact, smile, and (firm, warm, and dry) handshake. If you have not already done so, express your desire for the job. If you have not yet provided your references, hand the interviewer your references sheet. Tell him when you can start work and ask for an agreeable date to follow up on the hiring decision.

Follow-up Options

Let the interviewer define the rules for this last strategy. Ask him for an agreeable date and time to call about the hiring decision. If he states explicitly that he will call you or that he prefers not to receive thank-you letters, then respect his wishes. You do not want to annoy an employer right before he makes a hiring decision.

Take notes immediately after your interview (out of the employer's sight) to ensure your follow-up efforts are accurate. Record specific names, dates, procedures, resources, or other examples of common ground. The following are some ways to discuss your desire for the job or reinforce the positive points established during your meeting:

- Letter (sometimes called a thank-you note). This is an effective way to summarize the meeting, remind the interviewer of your name, and restate your hope to be hired. Your letter will be most effective if kept brief. Faxing it may be an assertive choice, but you should always mail the original after you have sent it by facsimile machine. See example.

SAMPLE FOLLOW-UP LETTER

RICH D. ZIRE, CPC
100-K Bank Alley
Washington, DC 20007
(202) 555-1001

July 8, 1992

Steward F. Winter, Senior Advisor
The Very Established Investment and Trust
A-1 Constitution Avenue, NW
Washington, DC 20006

RE: Retirement Portfolio Manager

Dear Mr. Winter:

I appreciate your time and attention during our July 7 meeting regarding the management position. I want to reiterate my ambition to work for your firm. I believe my experience with progressive financial practices will serve to continue your successful reputation.

I hope to hear from you soon regarding a second interview as I am eager to meet more of the management team. I am confident we could negotiate a mutually acceptable employment package. Again, thank you for the opportunity.

Warm regards,

Rich D. Zire

Rich D. Zire, CPC

RDZ

- Telephone Call—If the interviewer gives you a specific date and time to call, set your alarm clock, write it in your date book, or tell your friends to remind you. Do whatever you must to ensure you make the call. This is the last question on the test. You must prove you are dependable.
- Visit—Do not drop by or try to schedule an appointment unless explicitly requested by the interviewer. The next meeting may be the second interview, a chance to meet the big boss or review a contract. Since you definitely do not have the job at this point, accommodate the interviewer's instructions.
- Gifts—Presents are not a good idea. Even if you are applying for a marketing job or another kind of professional schmoozing, gifts dispensed before money-related decisions are bribery. Flattery, on the other hand, is free.

The follow-up stage is the most important part in refining your research findings. If an employer does not hire you, make a brief call to the interviewer to ask for some constructive feedback. Instead of criticizing his judgement, ask how you rated compared to your competition. It may be your salary requirement was too high, or your experience with a specific technology or technique was not as impressive as another candidates'. If you let him know you are still interested in working for the company and you want to build your qualifications in with company objectives, he will likely give you some helpful advice.

Miscellaneous Points

Variations on the interview strategies described here occur when you meet with your employer over promotions or you visit a job fair. Hopefully, you will not attend a job fair where your current boss has reserved the corner booth. In any event, interviewing with your upper-level managers is much the same as a new employer, but you have the benefit of inside information in this situation.

If you truly value your company and your loyalty is genuine, tell them and reinforce it with specific examples. If you want to renegotiate perquisites, frame them under the promise to increase productivity and efficiency; present the increased cost as a sound investment. Be patient. The old guard usually does not put extra pennies toward your car phone when they could spend the funds on their own options.

A job fair is an exciting and efficient way to look for work. Employers usually advertise them in the classifieds, job service offices, and campus career service centers. The Office of Personnel Management coordinates federal job fairs. When you identify a job fair, review the list of employers attending. See if any literature is available on the companies and jobs descriptions of openings. You may find out this information from the job fair coordinator. Otherwise, you have much work to do before attending. The only distinguishing factor in job fair interviews is that they are usually much shorter, so you should be prepared to pitch your qualifications quickly.

Suppose you receive several job offers. In Washington, it is common for people to work two jobs, but not two full-time jobs. You cannot serve two masters. Whichever employer you pick, be sure not to lead on the others unnecessarily. If one job does not work out, it is important to have other contacts. If, unfortunately, you have not garnered any jobs, keep your chin up and your suit dry-cleaned. If you are persistent and learn from interviews, you will soon have a job that satisfies you and the employer.

Do not be surprised if the hiring process takes several weeks or even several months. After hiring officers screen out applications, contact several candidates for interviews, work the meetings into their schedule, and complete the interviews and reference checks, they may offer the job to someone who may take a week to decide. If he declines, they may offer it to another, who may start and then take another job. Meanwhile, two other applicants have called to follow up—twice each—and have learned the officers are still considering "unforeseeable factors." This is a normal scenario.

The season in which you apply can affect the hiring process as well. Summer vacations and end-of-year holidays hinder nearly all business productivity. The absence of key company decision-makers can delay certain stages for weeks, not to mention decisions based on fiscal timing. If you are smart and have prepared for every job search stage, be patient and keep looking. If a certain job is your first choice, let the hiring officers know. Also, keep your fingers crossed that your competitors have not bought this book.

Summary

You have been through the whole interviewing process. Now, you are ready to rehearse your interview technique, ideally with someone who will not leak your job search to your current employer. Someone who serves as your professional reference is an excellent choice. If you know you really need help, contact the career services office of your alma mater or your state job service, or hire an employment counselor. When it comes to cultivating your livelihood, give it the attention and effort it deserves.

Appendix A
EMPLOYMENT RESOURCES

The following resources are available through area public libraries or bookstores.

Covin, Carol. *Covin's Washington Area Computer Job Guide*. Arlington: Vandamere Press, 1992.

Fitzpatrick, William G., and C. Edward Good. *Does Your Résumé Wear Combat Boots? Successful Transition from Military Life: A Jobseeker's Guide*. Charlottesville: Blue Jeans Press, 1990.

Lauber, Daniel. *The Compleat Guide to Finding Government Jobs*. River Forest: Planning Communications, 1989.

Milloy, John T. *Dress for Success*. Second edition. New York: Warner Books, 1978.

Murphy, Kevin J. *Surviving the Cut*. New York: Bantam Books, 1991.

Parker, Yana. *The Résumé Catalog—200 Damn Good Examples*. Berkeley: Ten Speed Press, 1988.

Rushlow, Ed. *Get A Better Job!* Princeton: Peterson's Guides, 1990.

Savage, Kathleen M., and Charity Anne Dorgan, editors. *Professional Careers Sourcebook, an Informational Guide for Career Planning*. Detroit: Gale Research, Inc., 1990.

Waelde, David E. *How to Get a Federal Job*. Washington, DC: Fedhelp Publications, 1990.

Yeager, Neil, and Lee Hough. *Power Interviews—Job Winning Tactics from Fortune 500 Companies*. New York: Wiley and Sons, Inc., 1990.

The following directories are helpful in researching employers.

American Directory Publishing. *Virginia Business Directory*. Omaha, NE, 1990. Organized by "yellow page" category, city and product, and by city.

American Society of Association Executives. *Who's Who in Association Management*. Washington, DC, 1990. ASAE's official membership directory.

Columbia Books. *National Trade and Professional Associations of the United States*. Washington, DC, 1990. Lists all associations by name, address, size, budget, and contacts. Has cross-referenced indices for location, subject, name, budget, and acronym.

Contacts Influential. *Northern Virginia Marketing Directory*. Portland, OR, 1990. Organized by company name, industry, zip code, "key contacts," and telephone number.

Contacts Influential. *Washington DC Marketing Directory*. Portland, OR, 1989. For the District and surrounding Maryland suburbs; organized by company name, industry, zip code, "key contacts," and telephone number.

Corporate Technology Information Services, Inc. *Maryland High-Tech Directory*. Woburn, MA, 1990. Organized by total employees, company profile, city, and product.

Dun's Marketing Services, Inc. *Dun's Regional Business Directory*. Parsippany, NJ, 1991. A comparison of local industry, public and private: business type, contact names, sales volume, parent companies, and number of employees.

Fairfax County Public Libraries. *Using the Library for Job Hunting*. Updated yearly; provides information on using the Fairfax County library system for employer and job-seeking skills research.

Manufacturers' News. *Maryland Manufacturers' Directory*. Chicago, IL, 1990. Separate listings for Chambers of Commerce, manufacturers by county, total employees, industry, Standard Industrial Classification, and alphabet.

Virginia Chamber of Commerce. *Virginia Industrial Directory*. Richmond, VA, 1990. Includes manufacturing and mining listings (by product, company name, and location), utilities, airlines, railroads, higher education, and foreign consulates.

The following are computer job search resources found in software retailers.

The Better Working Résumé Kit has options for different occupational groups.

The Individual Résumé Maker is recommended for experienced workers with longer employment histories.

Quick and Easy for the SF-171 can be purchased for one or two applicants' use. It can be printed directly on the original green form, or the form can be reproduced entirely by a laser printer.

The following are companies that sell job vacancy listings.

Education Week, at (202) 686-0800, for education administrative vacancies as well as some teaching positions.

The Federal Jobs Digest, at (800) 824-5000.

Federal Reports, at (202) 393-3311.

Federal Research Service, Inc., at (202) 333-5627 or (800) 822-5627.

Appendix B
GOVERNMENT JOBLINES

This appendix is a directory of government offices using jobline telephone numbers. This is not a comprehensive government listing. The employers here are listed alphabetically with their addresses, jobline numbers, and short descriptions. Common employer acronyms are also provided for reference. Although some employers listed do not use joblines, they are included because they have regular openings. Local Job Service offices are also listed.

ACTION—The National Volunteer Agency

Personnel
1100 Vermont Avenue, NW
Washington, DC 20525
(202) 634-1000

ACTION is the federal domestic volunteer outreach agency, essentially the domestic Peace Corps. Action's programs include VISTA, foster grandparents, and substance abuse intervention. They employ clerical, legal, professional, administrative, educational, and human services personnel. A security clearance is required for some jobs. Use an SF-171 to apply. Jobs are located in Washington, DC, and nationally. Action's headquarters are located near the McPherson Square Metro Station. Contact Personnel directly at (202) 634-9263. The TDD number is (202) 634-9256; the fax number is (202) 634-9182.

Agricultural Research Service

US Department of Agriculture
Personnel
6305 Ivy Lane, Room 106
Greenbelt, MD 20770-1435
(301) 344-2288

ARS is the principal scientific national research facility for the US Department of Agriculture, employing high-level chemistry, biology, and engineering professionals, as well as clerical, administrative, technical, library, and accounting support. A security clearance is required for some jobs. Use an SF-171 to apply. Jobs are located at the Beltsville Research Farm, in Washington, DC, and nationally. Call Personnel for more information at (301) 344-1124. The TDD number is 344-1124.

Agriculture, US Department of

Central Personnel
Independence Avenue and 14th Street, SW
Washington, DC 20250
(202) 447-5625

USDA is a federal department encompassing 17 different agencies concerned with animal and plant agricultural research, development, and distribution. Central Personnel does not hire directly, but refers applicants to appropriate agencies. The Agricultural Research Service (see above) has its own jobline. USDA employs many clerical, student, technical, and professional personnel. USDA has offices in Washington, Maryland, and Virginia. An SF-171 and photograph identification are required to apply. The Personnel office is located near the Smithsonian Metro Station. Clerical testing is on Tuesdays, 8 a.m. and 11 a.m., Room 1080. Applications are accepted Monday, Wednesday, Thursday, and Friday from 8 a.m. to 2 p.m. The TDD numbers are (202) 447-2436 and (202) 447-6905. Personnel can be contacted directly at (202) 447-2436.

Air Force District of Washington

Civilian Personnel Office
5-E-871 Pentagon
Washington, DC 20330-6420
(703) 693-6550 (touch-tone)

x1—general job information
x2—job listings
x3—Air Force merit promotions
x4—special employment
x5—application checking
x6—benefits and services
x9—nonappropriated employment
x0—repeat sequence

This office is a civilian employment center for the support of the US Air Force in the Washington, DC, area, including Bolling Air Force Base. Occupations include computer, clerical, technical, graphic, accounting, intelligence, and administrative, and span all federal "GS" salary grades. Andrews Air Force Base has its own jobline listed in this book. Civilian jobs are located in Washington, Maryland, Virginia, nationally, and overseas. Some jobs require a security clearance. An SF-171 is required to apply. The main personnel office is located near the Pentagon Metro Station and can be called directly at (703) 695-4389 or (703) 695-4582. The TDD number is (703) 693-7389.

Alcohol, Drug Abuse, and Mental Health Administration

Department of Health and Human Services
Room 15-C-12
5600 Fisher's Lane
Rockville, MD 20857
(301) 443-2282

This is the federal agency governing research and implementation of mental illness and substance abuse treatment. This listing also includes associated facilities. They employ social service, computer, and statistical professionals, and support and administrative personnel. Jobs are located in Rockville, near the Twinbrook Metro Station, and in Bethesda and Baltimore. An SF-171 is required to apply. Call Personnel at (301) 443-5407. To request a vacancy announcement, call (301) 443-9071. The TDD number is (301) 443-5437.

Alcohol, Tobacco, and Firearms, Bureau of US Department of the Treasury

Room 1216
1200 Pennsylvania Avenue, NW
Washington, DC 20226

ATF is the federal bureau enforcing and regulating the sales, manufacture, and taxation of controlled substances. They employ inspectors, law enforcement agents, investigators, chemists, auditors, technicians, administrators, clerks, and managers. A security clearance is required. The main office is near the Federal Triangle Metro Station. Some travel may be required for professional positions. An SF-171 is required to apply. Call Employment at (202) 566-7321. The TDD number is (202) 535-6330.

Alexandria, City of

Personnel Services Department
City Hall, Room 2500
301 King Street
Alexandria, VA 22314
(703) 838-4422 (touch-tone)
x0000—operator
x8888—job listings
x9999—application

Alexandria is a municipal district located immediately south of Arlington, VA, and Washington, DC, inside the Capital Beltway west of the Potomac River. The city employs a wide variety of entry-level labor and administrative positions and professionals. The main office is near the King Street Metro Station. When listening to the jobline, write down the four-digit job number and use it as an extension number to listen to more information about that vacancy. A city application is required, and must be received by the vacancy closing date. The TDD number is (703) 838-5035, and you can reach Personnel at (703) 838-4423.

Alexandria City Public Schools

Personnel Office
3801 West Braddock Road
Alexandria, VA 22302
(703) 758-4008 (touch-tone)
x1—administrative
x2—teaching
x3—support
x4—general

This educational system serves the city of Alexandria, VA. They advertise all vacancies on the jobline, including teachers, educational specialists, librarians, aides, and maintenance and clerical workers. Applicants must record the vacancy announcement number on the application as listed on the jobline. All clerical applicants must schedule a testing appointment before interviewing. Call Personnel at (703) 824-6665, and the fax number is (703) 820-8491.

Andrews Air Force Base

Civilian Personnel
Headquarters
89 MSSQ
Airlift Wing/MSCA
Washington, DC 20331-5964
(301) 981-5431

Home of Air Force One, this facility supports the US President, the Air Force, the Air National Guard, and the Navy. Civil Service includes clerical, trades, engineering, administrative, and professional positions. AAFB is independent of the Air Force District of Washington and coordinates jobs in Maryland and Virginia. An SF-171 is required to apply. The Civilian Personnel Office is open from 9:00 a.m.-3:00 p.m. in Building 1413, Room 329. Applicants without a government or military pass must enter the Visitor Information Center and ask for a temporary pass. For more information, call Personnel at (301) 981-4581.

Arlington County

Personnel
2100 Clarendon Boulevard
Suite 511
Arlington, VA 22201
(703) 538-3363 (touch-tone)
x8888—job listings
x9999—applications

Arlington is a Virginia municipality southwest of Washington, DC, on the Potomac River. The county employs general government personnel, including clerical, trades, and administration. You must use a county application for specific job vacancies. The Personnel office is near Courthouse Metro Station. They can be reached at (703) 358-3500, the fax number is (703) 358-3903, and the TDD number is (703) 358-4613.

Arlington County Public Schools

Personnel
1426 North Quincy Street
Arlington, VA 22207
(703) 358-6100, x0

This office coordinates employment for the Arlington school system. They are open from 7:30 a.m. to 4:30 p.m. They accept applications for openings and to keep on file. Call (703) 358-6101 for teacher applications and (703) 358-6100 for more information. The fax number is (703) 358-6188.

Arms Control and Disarmament Agency

Personnel
320 21st Street, NW
Washington, DC 20451

ACDA was created by Congress in 1961 to implement international arms policy and to promote national security. They work closely with the State

Department. They hire computer, clerical, and foreign affairs specialists. Professional-level applicants should have at least a master's degree. An SF-171 is required. Personnel will keep applications of qualified candidates. All employees must pass a security clearance. The office is near the Foggy Bottom Metro Station, and can be reached at (202) 647-2034. The fax number is (202) 647-6721, and fax confirmation is at (202) 647-8666.

Army, Department of

US Total Army Personnel Command
Attention: TAPC-CPF-S
200 Stovall Street
Alexandria, VA 22332-0341
(703) 325-2034

This office coordinates Army civilian overseas jobs only for all kinds of civilian work. An SF-171 is required; the form is sent to the location of the job opening, not the Stovall Street office. They are located near the Eisenhower Metro Station. If you have a security clearance, job listings can be reviewed in the office. For more information, call (703) 325-9228.

Census, Bureau of the

US Department of Commerce
Personnel Division
Room 1412, Building 3
Washington, DC 20233
(301) 763-6064 (touch-tone)
x1—clerical testing
x2—directions
x3—job listings

This federal bureau is the national statistical data gathering and analysis agency. They employ professional, clerical, managerial, and wage grade workers, especially statisticians. A security clearance is required for most positions. Jobs are located in Suitland, MD, and nationally. An SF-171 is required to apply; a college transcript may also be required. The TDD number is (301) 763-4494. Call Personnel directly at (301) 763-6064, x4; (301) 763-7470; or (800) 638-6719.

Central Intelligence Agency

Personnel Representative
PO Box 12727
Arlington, VA 22209-8727

This is the agency coordinating services of US government intelligence. The CIA hires degreed professionals for clerical, professional, high-tech, and computer jobs. The CIA has offices in Virginia and Washington, DC. Applicants must use a résumé instead of SF-171. For more information, call Personnel at (703) 351-2141.

Commerce, US Department of

Office of Personnel Operations
14th Street and Constitution Avenue, NW
Room 1069
Washington, DC 20230
(202) 377-4285
(202) 377-5138 (touch-tone)

x3—GS 2-6	x7—wage grade positions
x4—GS 7-9	x8—addresses of agencies
x5—GS 11-12	x9—application status
x6—GS 13 +	

This federal department regulates domestic and foreign trade. The jobline provides information on applying to the various US Department of Commerce agencies and bureaus. Jobs are located in Washington, Maryland, Virginia, and nationally. The main office is near the Federal Triangle Metro Station. The main office is an excellent resource for reviewing vacancy announcements for all agencies within the department. An SF-171 if required to apply; however, they do not accept applications but refer applicants to the appropriate agency's personnel office.

Commodity Futures Trading Commission

Personnel
2033 K Street, NW
Suite 202
Washington, DC 20581
(202) 254-3346

CFTC is a regulatory agency for commodities. They hire investigators, officers, attorneys, clerks, financial analysts, and other related professionals. Jobs are located in Washington, DC (near the Farragut North and West, and Foggy Bottom Metro Stations), and nationally. An SF-171 is required to apply. To request a vacancy announcement, leave your name and address, and the vacancy announcement number after the message tone. For more information, call Personnel at (202) 254-3275.

Consolidated Civilian Personnel Office

Department of the Navy
Crystal City
Crystal Mall #2, Room 424
Code 133
Washington, DC 20376-5006
(703) 692-4133

This CCPO is the Virginia hiring office for the Department of the Navy for such occupations as high-level management, engineering, professional, accounting, clerical, computer, architects, and support. All jobs require a security clearance. Jobs are located in Virginia and Washington, DC. Some vacancies from the Washington Navy Yard are also included; however, the Pentagon is not. To request an SF-171 and vacancy announcement, leave your name and address after the jobline tone. The CCPO is near the Crystal City Metro Station. Call personnel at (703) 692-4139. The TDD number is (703) 692-2658.

Courts, US

Administrative Office
1120 Vermont Avenue, NW
Suite 1008
Washington, DC 20544
(202) 633-6061

The US Court is the level of the federal judiciary system just below the Supreme Court. The jobline advertises only local openings in administration, computers, paralegal, and clerical jobs. Some positions require a security clearance. An SF-171 is required. The main office is near the McPherson Square Metro Station. Call personnel at (202) 633-6116.

Customs Service

Treasury Department
Human Resources
Box # (see below)
Washington, DC 20044
or
1311 Constitution Avenue, NW
Washington, DC 20044
(202) 566-8195 (touch-tone)
x1—job listings

The Customs Service is the federal agency regulating the flow of materials in and out of the country. They employ people in computers, clerical, agents, professional, administrative, support, management, investigation, aviation, accounting, financial, legal, and technical positions. A security clearance and drug screening are required. Jobs are located in Washington, Virginia, Maryland, and nationally. Send an SF-171 to the appropriate box numbers as listed below.

Admissions Support—Box #7537
Operations—Box #7747
Executive Services—Box #636
Enforcement—Box #6128

Human Resources is located near the Federal Triangle Metro Station and can be reached at (202) 634-5155 for jobs in the Washington metropolitan area.

Defense Communications Agency

see Defense Information Systems Agency

Defense Information Systems Agency

Code BCEE
701 South Courthouse Road
Arlington, VA 22204-2199
(703) 746-1724

DISA's mission is to ". . . plan, engineer, develop, test, implement, operate, and maintain joint information systems in support of national security as directed." They employ computer, engineering, clerical, and administrative workers. Jobs are located in Reston and Sterling, VA, and Washington, DC. An SF-171 and a security clearance are required. Call personnel at (703) 692-2783.

Defense Intelligence Agency

Attention: RHR-2
Department TM
3100 Clarendon Boulevard
Arlington, VA 22201-5322
(703) 284-1110

The DIA produces and analyzes intelligence for national policy officials and manages Department of Defense programs. They recruit for clerical, technical, computer, officer, administrative, professional, mechanical, and teaching positions. All applicants must pass a thorough background check and drug testing to qualify for hiring. An SF-171 is required to apply. The office is located near the Courthouse Metro Station. Call (703) 284-1321 to request a vacancy announcement; call (703) 284-1124/1321 to reach Civilian Staffing. The TDD number is (703) 284-1082.

Defense Logistics Agency

CPO, Room 6-214
Cameron Station
Alexandria, VA 22304-6130
(703) 274-7372

The DLA is the federal agency responsible for buying standard items for all military components. They offer entry- to top-level positions, including clerical, logistical, supply management, transportation management, and contract administration. They have employees throughout the world; jobs are located locally in Virginia. Some require a security clearance. An SF-171 is required to apply. The TDD number is (703) 274-6287. Personnel can be reached at (703) 274-7087.

District of Columbia Government

Central Job Information Center
613 G Street, NW
Suite 301
Washington, DC 20001
(202) 727-6099 (touch-tone)
x2—clerical
x0—operator

The city of Washington's main personnel office no longer publishes a job bulletin but displays job listings at the Center. It is open from 8:15 a.m. to 4:45 p.m., and is near the Gallery Place Metro Station. From the listings, you may request vacancy announcements that provide further application information. The District uses SF-171s, which is the same form used by the federal government; it can be mailed or delivered to the appropriate office. The Center, however, does not accept or distribute applications. Applications are sometimes kept on file during any hiring freeze. Candidates must be District residents or future residents to be hired. The TDD number is (202) 347-5509.

District of Columbia Government

Department of Employment Services
1217 Good Hope Road, SE
Washington, DC 20020
(202) 767-8300

25 K Street, NE
Washington, DC 20002
(202) 724-2316

4017 Minnesota Avenue, NE
Washington, DC 20019
(202) 727-4861

8th and Xenia Streets, SE
Washington, DC 20032
(202) 767-8129

4120 Kansas Avenue, NW
Washington, DC 20011
(202) 576-7450

1000 U Street, NW
Washington, DC 20001
(202) 673-6591

Latino Center
1803 Belmont Road, NW
Washington, DC 20009
(202) 673-6634

The District's Job Service Offices are located throughout the city. They offer information and assistance on job-seeking skills, employment training, a job bank, unemployment compensation, workers' compensation, and veterans' services. The main information number is (202) 639-2000.

District of Columbia Public Schools

Division of Personnel Services
415 12th Street, NW
Suite 706
Washington, DC 20004
(202) 724-4054

The District's public schools Personnel is part of the District's central personnel office, but they also coordinate their own hiring of teachers and nonteaching staff. It is open 8:00 a.m. to 4:30 p.m., and is near the Federal Triangle Metro Station. They also use SF-171s, but teachers and school officers must complete separate applications. Candidates must be District residents or future residents. Schools are not affected during hiring freezes. The TDD number is (202) 724-4054. The teacher recruiter can be reached at (800) TEACH-DC [(800) 832-2432]. For more information, call Personnel at (202) 724-4080.

Drug Enforcement Administration

see Justice, US Department of

Education, US Department of

Personnel Division, Room 1156
400 Maryland Avenue, SW
Washington, DC 20202

This federal department governs the policies and practices of state public school systems. They have entry-level up to director-level positions. Openings are designated as being available to the general public, federal employees, and department employees. They often have clerical, computer, accounting, statistics, management, educational, and rehabilitation vacancies. Jobs are located at the main office, which is near the L'Enfant Plaza Metro Station, and nationally. An SF-171 is required. Apply in person to review job descriptions. Call Personnel at (202) 401-0559 for more information.

Energy, US Department of

Personnel Office
1000 Independence Avenue, SW
Washington, DC 20585
(202) 586-4333 (touch-tone)

This agency is the developer, producer, and supplier of nuclear materials for national security. They employ entry- to top-level engineering, clerical, administrative, computer, mathematics, accounting, trades, scientific, investigative, and intelligence personnel. Jobs are located in Washington, DC, and Maryland. Some require a security clearance. The main office is near the Smithsonian Metro Station. An SF-171 is required. There is TDD access to all telephone numbers except the jobline. Personnel can be reached at (202) 586-8580.

Environmental Protection Agency

Employment Services
401 M Street, SW
Washington, DC 20460
(202) 755-5055

The EPA protects the nation's environment. They employ clerical, support, administrative, scientific, computer, engineering, and activist personnel. Jobs are located in Washington, DC (near the L'Enfant Plaza Metro Station), and Arlington, VA (near the Crystal City Metro Station). An SF-171 is required to apply. For more information, call Employment Services at (202) 382-3144. The TDD number is (202) 382-3141.

Executive Office of the President

Office of Administration
725 17th Street, NW
Room 4013
Washington, DC 20503
(202) 395-5892

This office coordinates hiring for 16 agencies within the new and old Executive office buildings, the "foundation of the federal government." Opportunities may include financial, research, technical, and clerical work. The buildings are near the Farragut North and West Metro Stations. An SF-171 is required to apply. The Personnel office recommends that applicants request a vacancy announcement after the jobline tone and then forward the SF-171 by mail. They prefer not to receive direct telephone calls.

Export-Import Bank of the US

Human Resources
811 Vermont Avenue, NW
Washington, DC 20571
(202) 389-1172

The Eximbank is an independent federal agency that facilitates export financing of US goods and services. Jobs that may be available are loan specialist, financial analyst, computer professional, accountant, attorney, economist, and clerical and administrative workers. An SF-171 is required; a security clearance is required for some jobs. The office is near the McPherson Square Metro Station and can be reached at (202) 566-8834. The TDD number is (202) 535-3913.

Fairfax, City of

Personnel Department
10455 Armstrong Street
Fairfax, VA 22030
(703) 385-7860

The city of Fairfax is a municipal area located entirely within Fairfax County, VA, outside the Capital Beltway. The city employs support, service, labor, law enforcement, and other professional workers. Personnel accepts only City of Fairfax applications, and they are not kept on file after vacancies are filled. Preference is given to city residents and current employees for job openings. Fairfax County Public Schools coordinate hiring for schools in Fairfax City. To request an application, call (703) 385-7939. For more information, call Personnel at (703) 385-7861. The fax number is (703) 385-7811.

Fairfax, County of

Office of Personnel
4103 Chain Bridge Road
Suite 100
Fairfax, VA 22030
(703) 246-4600 (touch-tone)

The county of Fairfax surrounds, but does not include, the city of Fairfax. It is a large municipal area of Virginia, spanning the Potomac River shore west and south of Washington, and southwest of Arlington, Alexandria, and Falls Church. The county employs administrative, professional, labor, technical, legal, scientific, engineering, accounting, computer, recreation, clerical, and social service personnel. The TDD number is (703) 934-1298; the fax number is (703) 352-8680. There is also a job listings bulletin posted in Job Service offices and libraries; it can also be requested by mail. A county application must be used for all vacancies; these are not kept on file once the vacancies are filled. For more information call the Application Center at (703) 591-8560 or Personnel at (703) 246-3448.

Fairfax County Public Schools

Department of Personnel Services
6815 Edsall Road
Springfield, VA 22151
(703) 750-8400 (touch-tone)
(703) 750-8533 (support jobs)

Fairfax County Public Schools operate a touch-tone jobline menu, listing educational, substitute, support, custodial, technical, and management positions by a series of touch-tone codes. You can also request an application by leaving your name and address at the end of the message. Hiring includes the City of Fairfax schools. You may contact Personnel during business hours at (703) 750-8400, requesting the operator.

Falls Church, City of

Personnel
300 Park Avenue
Falls Church, VA 22046
(703) 241-5130, x143 (touch-tone)

Falls Church is a small jurisdiction in Virginia, bordering Fairfax and Arlington counties. The city employs clerical, maintenance, recreation, law enforcement, and service personnel. A city application is required. The Falls Church Public Schools office does not have a jobline, but it can be contacted at (703) 241-7600. Call City Personnel directly at (703) 241-5025. The fax number is (703) 241-5184; the TDD number is (703) 241-5149.

Federal Aviation Administration

Department of Transportation
Employment Branch AHR-150
800 Independence Avenue, SW
Washington, DC 20591
(202) 267-3902 (touch-tone)

x1—clerical
x2—mid-level nonsupervisory
x3—aviation and engineering
x4—managerial

x5—local requiring federal status
x6—national requiring federal
    status
x0—operator
x*—repeat previous sequence

FAA coordinates United States' aviation services. They employ the personnel listed above in Washington, DC, including air traffic controllers. An SF-171 is required to apply. FAA's main office is near the L'Enfant Plaza Metro Station. For more information, call Human Resources Management at (202) 267-8007 and wait for the end of the jobline message.

Federal Bureau of Investigation

see Justice, US Department of

Federal Deposit Insurance Corporation

Personnel
550 17th Street, NW
Washington, DC 20429-9990
or
Job Information Center
1776 G Street, NW
Suite 4000
Washington, DC 20006
(202) 898-8890/1 (touch-tone)
x1—to request forms
x2—to access a personal extension
x3—job listings
    x1—temporary assignments
    x2—independent contracts
    x3—jobs outside DC
    x4—jobs inside DC
    x7—repeat menu
    x8—return to main menu
x4—information about FDIC and RTC
x5—TDD
x7—repeat menu
(800) 424-4334, x88890 (accesses above extensions)

FDIC regulates and supervises banks to ensure compliance with regulations and adherence to banking principles. FDIC includes the Resolution Trust Corporation, which was created in 1989 to resolve failed savings and loan firms. They hire legal, computer, financial management, accounting, auditing, secretarial, clerical, administrative, wage grade, management, and financial analysis workers. An SF-171 and other forms per vacancy announcement are required. They accept applications for specific vacancies only. Both offices are near the Farragut West Metro Station. Mail applications to the 17th Street address. Walk-in information is available at the G Street address. For more information, call (202) 898-8890/1, x4, then x4, then x3, then x1, and ask for an information specialist.

Federal Energy Regulatory Commission

810 First Street, NE
Suite 418
Washington, DC 20426
(202) 219-2791

FERC enforces the Department of Energy's standards. They employ clerical, supervisory, accounting, engineering, computer, and support personnel. Jobs are located in Washington, DC, and nationally. They perform a background check on all applicants. An SF-171 is required to apply. The main office is near the Union Station Metro Station. Personnel can be reached at (202) 219-2990.

Federal Home Loan Bank Board

Human Resources
1700 G Street, NW
Washington, DC 20552
(202) 906-7223

This agency regulates the nation's home loans. The jobline advertises clerical, management, legal, accounting, and support positions. Jobs are located in Washington, DC, and nationally. An SF-171 is required to apply. The main office is near Farragut West Metro Station. For more information, call Human Resources at (202) 906-6060.

Federal Job Information Center

Office of Personnel Management
Financial, Administrative, and Social Services Recruiting
1900 E Street, NW
Room 1416
Washington, DC 20415
(202) 606-2700 (touch-tone)

x1—general job information
x2—job description requests
x3—walk in testing information
x4—job vacancy announcements
x5—to check application status

x6—veteran employment
  opportunities
x7—employee locator
x9—to repeat previous sequence
x0—operator

x409—job fairs

This office is a clearinghouse for local federal employment opportunities. Types of occupations include health, safety, medical, writing, public interest, business, financial, administrative, computer, legal, law enforcement, social service, Social Security, clerical, and senior executive service. The office coordinates hiring for Washington, Maryland, and Virginia. It is located near the Farragut West Metro Station. The TDD number is (202) 606-0591. Call Personnel at (202) 606-2700, x0.

Federal Reserve Board

Division of Human Resources Management
Board of Governors of the Federal Reserve System
20th and C Streets, NW
Mail Stop 156
Washington, DC 20551
(202) 452-3038

Governed by Congress, this agency oversees the economy and regulates 12 national reserve banks. They employ economists, attorneys, researchers, and computer programmers; and support, clerical, and maintenance personnel. The office is near the Foggy Bottom and Farragut West Metro Stations. Applicants may use a résumé or the Board's application. They perform a background check on all potential employees. Call Human Resources at (202) 452-3880 or (800) 448-4894.

Fish and Wildlife Service

Department of the Interior
Personnel Office
4401 North Fairfax Drive
Arlington, VA 22203
or
Personnel Office
1 Gateway Center
Suite 612
Newton Corner, MA 01258
(703) 358-2120 (touch-tone)

x1—request copy of announcement   x6—law enforcement
x2—job listing for Washington   x7—research and development
x3—addresses of personnel   x8—replay this sequence
x4—clerical   x9—return to main menu
x5—biology   x0—operator

This federal office serves and protects fish and wildlife, especially endangered species, with fisheries, game preserves, and other assistance. They employ professionals as listed above. To apply for research and development jobs, send an SF-171 to the Virginia address using Room 725, or call (703) 358-1771. For Washington, DC, vacancies and GS-14 and above, send an SF-171 to the Virginia address using Room 100, or call (703) 358-1743. It is near the Ballston Metro Station. For Maryland and Virginia vacancies, send an SF-171 to the Massachusetts address or call (617) 965-5100, x239.

Food and Drug Administration

Department of Health and Human Services
5600 Fisher's Lane
Room 4-B-41
Rockville, MD 20857
(301) 443-1969

FDA is responsible for approving all new food additives, drugs, cosmetics, and devices. FDA is located in more than 24 sites with 5000 employees in the Washington metropolitan area. Plans are being studied for consolidation in one campus in the near future. FDA also regulates the Public Health Service, which has its own jobline. FDA employs clerical and support workers, chemists, biologists, engineers, accountants, and computer professionals. The facility is near the Twinbrook Metro Station. An SF-171 is required to apply. Call personnel at (301) 443-1970, which is also equipped for TDD.

Fort Meade

One Stop Employment Information Center
Building 4283
Fort Meade, MD 20755-5036
(301) 677-4473

Fort Meade is a US Army base between Washington and Baltimore. It is the Army's East Coast civilian employment headquarters for 6000 employees. It offers maintenance, medical, clerical, administrative, technical, and Army Reserve opportunities. Some Fort Ritchie vacancies are included; however, see Fort Ritchie below for more specific information. The National Security Agency, while located at Fort Meade, is a separate entity. Jobs listed are located in Maryland, Virginia, and nationally. An SF-171 is required to apply.

You may take your SF-171 form to Fort Meade in person Monday - Thursday, 8:00 a.m.-3:00 p.m. There are monthly clerical screening tests as well. For more information, call personnel at (301) 677-6846.

Fort Ritchie

Department of the Army
HQ US Army Garrison Fort Ritchie
Attention: Civilian Personnel Office
ASQNJ-CP
Fort Ritchie, MD 21719-5010
(301) 878-5264

Fort Ritchie is an Army communications installation north of Frederick, MD, along the Pennsylvania border. The jobline advertises such positions as clerical, communications, management, technical, administrative, warehouse, computer, and support. These opportunities are available only at Fort Ritchie. An SF-171, SF-50, and performance appraisal are required since most of the vacancies are for Civil Service status candidates. All require a security clearance. For nonfederal positions, call (301) 878-5573. For more information, call Personnel at (301) 878-5265.

General Accounting Office

Office of Recruitment
441 G Street, NW
Room 1050
Washington, DC 20548
(202) 275-6092 (touch-tone)
x2—job listings
x3—check application status
x4—general information
x5—college relations questions
x6—repeat this sequence

GAO is the federal accounting office that assembles and checks the country's financial information. They employ accountants, evaluators, computer specialists, writers, economists, librarians, secretaries, administrators, social service and communications professionals, and summer interns. The building is near the Judiciary Square Metro Station. An SF-171 is required to apply. Clerical testing is required for GS levels 2-6. For more information, call (202) 275-6092, x1.

Geological Survey, US

Department of the Interior
12201 Sunrise Valley Drive
Mail Stop 215
Reston, VA 22092
(703) 648-7676 (touch-tone)
x1—clerical and technical
x2—professional
x3—administrative
x4—GS-14 and above

This federal office coordinates geological services for the country. They hire physicists, hydrologists, geologists, accountants, cartographers, computer and administrative professionals, and clerical workers. You may request a vacancy announcement after the jobline tone, by stating your name and address, and the vacancy announcement number. Jobs listed are in Virginia, Washington, Baltimore, and nationally. An SF-171 is required. Government status applicants must also submit an SF-50 and "KASOCs" performance appraisal form. The TDD number is (703) 648-7788, the FTS number is 959-7676; personnel can be reached at (703) 648-6131.

George Mason University

Human Resources
4087 University Drive
Fairfax, VA 22030
(703) 993-2601

GMU is a well-rounded educational institution with over 18,000 students. They employ clerical, maintenance, security, supervisory, professional, technical, faculty, and medical personnel. Jobs are in Fairfax and Arlington. GMU's Law School is near the Ballston Metro Station. A Commonwealth of Virginia application is required. Job listings can also be reviewed at the Fenwick Library. Faculty applicants should contact individual departments directly. Human Resources can be reached at (703) 993-2600.

Goddard Space Flight Center

National Aeronautics and Space Administration
Employment Services Branch
Code 115
Greenbelt, MD 20771
(301) 286-5326

Part of the National Aeronautics and Space Administration, Goddard is an air and space research and test facility. It employs engineering, management, flight operations, clerical, support, and computer personnel. The jobline lists jobs at Goddard and the Wallops Island, VA, facility. An SF-171, SF-50, and performance appraisal are required to apply, since only federal status candidates are eligible. Some require a security clearance as well. For more information, call Employment at (301) 286-7918, which is also TDD accessible.

Health Care Policy and Research, Agency for

see Public Health Service

Health, Office of the Assistant Secretary for

see Public Health Service

Health Resources and Services Administration

Department of Health and Human Services
Division of Personnel
Room 14-A-46
5600 Fisher's Lane
Rockville, MD 20857
(301) 443-1230

This office governs the nation's health care providers. It includes four bureaus: Health Care Delivery and Assistance, Health Professions, Maternal/Child Health, and Health Resources Development. The jobline advertises clerical and support positions and some professional vacancies. This is not a treatment facility. An SF-171, and a performance appraisal as applicable, are required. The office is near the Twinbrook Metro Station; it can be reached at (301) 443-5460, which is also TDD accessible.

House Placement Office

House Office Building
Annex II, Room 219
3rd x D Streets, SW
Washington, DC 20515

The House Placement Office serves as an application bank for any Congressional office, including House members and House Committee offices. The office keeps applications for 3 years, but applicants must contact them monthly to remain in their active file. Apply in person 10:30 a.m.-4:00 p.m. Monday—Friday. Bring your résumé, complete their application, take a typing test, and participate in an informational interview. Job vacancies may include receptionist, secretary, legislative assistant, legislative coordinator,

schedulist, caseworker, or professional staffer. The office is near the Federal
Center SW Metro Station. Call the staff at (202) 226-6731; the TDD number is (202) 225-6098.

Housing and Urban Development

Office of Personnel and Training
Room 2258
451 7th Street, SW
Washington, DC 20410-3100
(202) 708-3203 (touch-tone)

x1—job listings
x2—to request vacancy
  announcements
x3—working at HUD

x4—applying at HUD
x7—repeat this sequence
x8—repeat previous sequence

HUD regulates the nation's housing policies and practices. They employ
clerical, support, accounting, legal, supervisory, and equal housing opportunity specialists. They offer flex-time, a child care center, and a fitness
center. The office is near the L'Enfant Plaza Metro Station. An SF-171 is
required to apply; a supplemental statement of qualifications is recommended. For more information, call Personnel at (202) 708-0395, which is
also TDD accessible.

Howard County

Personnel
George Howard Building, First Floor
3430 Court House Drive
Ellicott City, MD 21043
(301) 313-2900 (touch-tone)
x9221—clerical openings
x9222—all others

Located southwest of Baltimore, MD, and north of Washington, DC, this
county government employs clerical, support, maintenance, recreation, and
professional workers, including firefighters, accountants, and police. You
must use the county's application. For more information, call Personnel at
(301) 313-2033. The TDD number is (301) 313-2323.

Howard County Schools

Personnel
10910 Route 108
Ellicott City, MD 21043
(301) 313-6643

This office coordinates the county's public school system. The jobline advertises support, clerical, and maintenance work, but does not list teachers or supervisors. For more information, call Personnel at (301) 313-6693. The TDD number is (301) 992-4942.

Immigration and Naturalization Service

Justice Department
Personnel Division
425 Eye Street, NW
Room 6023
Washington, DC 20536
(202) 514-4301

INS regulates the process of applying for United States' citizenship and its benefits under the Nationality Act. The jobline advertises legal, clerical, communications, security, accounting, support, service, and agent vacancies. Jobs are located at headquarters, near the Judiciary Square and Gallery Place Metro Stations, and nationally. The local office is in Arlington, VA, near the Ballston Metro Station. An SF-171 is required. Call Personnel at (202) 514-0136, which is also TDD accessible.

Indian Affairs, Bureau of

Department of the Interior
Branch of Personnel Services
Mail Stop 331-SIB
1951 Constitution Avenue, NW
Washington, DC 20245
(202) 208-2682

This bureau deals with issues related to native Americans, to whom employment preference is given. Vacancies may include clerk, inspector, appraiser, administrator, maintenance, accountant, educator, business, forestry, technician, and others. Jobs are located in Washington, DC, Arlington, VA, and nationally. An SF-171 is required. Personnel is located near the Farragut West Metro Station. For more information, call (202) 208-7581.

Information Agency, US

Office of Personnel
301 4th Street, SW
Room 518
Washington, DC 20547
(202) 619-4539

USIA receives, directs, develops, and analyzes information to advise the federal executive government branch on formulating foreign and domestic policy. The jobline advertises clerical, computer, languages, and support personnel for local and national openings. Employees must pass a security clearance to be hired. The office is near the Federal Center SW Metro Station. An SF-171, and SF-50 as applicable, are required to apply. For more information, call Personnel at (202) 619-4659.

Internal Revenue Service

Human Resources Branch
Room 1034
1111 Constitution Avenue, NW
Washington, DC 20224
(202) 535-5384 (touch-tone)
x16# to start jobline

The IRS collects and analyzes tax revenue and enforces federal tax law. They employ accounting, statistical, clerical, computer, security, legal, agent, investigative, and management personnel. Human Resources coordinates local hiring for Washington, DC, Maryland, and Virginia. It is near the Federal Triangle Metro Station. An SF-171 is required to apply. Call Human Resources at (202) 566-6151/3617.

Justice, US Department of

Justice Management Service
Personnel Staff
Room 402
(insert team number from tape)
633 Indiana Avenue, NW
Washington, DC 20530
(202) 514-6818

This office governs seven agencies dealing with prisons, drug enforcement, investigation, prosecution, and immigration. Refer also to individual agencies, bureaus, and offices for more information. The main jobline advertises clerical, legal, computer, language, support, and supervisory vacancies. An SF-171 is required. The Personnel office coordinates hiring for Washington, DC, Maryland, and Virginia. Near the Archives Metro Station, it can be reached at (202) 514-6877.

Labor, Department of

National Capital Service Center
200 Constitution Avenue, NW
Room C-5516
Washington, DC 20210
(202) 523-6646 (touch-tone)

x1—to access information
x1—how to apply
x2—special employment programs
x3—DC job listings
x4—outside DC job listings

The Department of Labor deals with all aspects of the country's employment from labor relations and safety to workers' compensation. They hire in many areas: clerical, investigation, legal, business, economics, accounting, computer, math, statistics, administration, budget, procurement, engineering, physical science, and industrial hygiene. An SF-171, US citizenship, and security clearance are required. To request a vacancy announcement, write down the DOL agency and vacancy announcement number and then call (202) 523-6677 or (800) 366-2753. The FTS number is 523-6646.

Library of Congress

Employment Office, Room LM-107
James Madison Memorial Building
101 Independence Avenue, SE
Washington, DC 20540
(202) 707-5295

This is the national library housing and regulating all copyrighted material. They often have library, research analysis, technical, clerical, computer, and assistant positions available. An SF-171 is required. For clerical and non-professional positions, a performance appraisal should be attached to the SF-171. Clerical tests are given Monday, Wednesday, and Friday at 8:45 a.m.; and Tuesday and Thursday at 8:45 a.m. and 2:00 p.m. Walk-in typing tests are given Monday—Friday, at 9:15 a.m. and 10:30 a.m.; and on Tuesday and Thursday at 2:30 p.m. Walk-in applications are accepted Monday—Friday, 8:30 a.m. to 4:30 p.m. Photograph identification is required at testing. The library is near the Capitol South Metro Station. For more information, call Employment at (202) 707-5627.

Loudoun, County of

Department of Human Resources
102 Heritage Way, NE
Suite 305
Leesburg, VA 22075
(703) 777-0536
(703) 478-8410 (metro line, ask for jobline)

The County of Loudoun is a Virginia locale west of Washington and Fairfax County. They often have openings in clerical, professional, and labor positions. Use the county's application, which you may request after the jobline tone. Loudoun County Public Schools has no jobline but can be contacted at (703) 771-6420. The TDD number is (703) 777-0107. Human Resources may be reached at (703) 777-0213 or (703) 478-8410 (metro line).

Marine Corps Headquarters

Civilian Personnel Branch
Code ARCA, Room 1215
Washington, DC 20380-0001
(703) 697-7474

This civilian personnel branch recruits candidates for Marine civilian vacancies, including those at Quantico the Pentagon, and Arlington. These vacancies may include clerical, maintenance, administrative, mechanical, engineering, and other professionals. Some vacancies are also advertised through other civilian personnel offices; however, this office coordinates hiring only for Virginia locations. An SF-171 is required. The Personnel office is near the Pentagon Metro Station and can be reached at (703) 614-1046 for more information and vacancy announcements.

Maryland-National Capital Park and Planning Commission

Employment and Testing Office
6609 Riggs Road
Hyattsville, MD 20782
(301) 927-5101 (touch-tone)
x3333—recreation programs for the disabled
x4444—aquatics jobs
x5555—summer employment
x7777—jobs open continuously
x8888—complete vacancy listing
x9999—to request a job application

MNCPPC maintains and develops the Washington and Maryland area parks. They employ recreation, service, maintenance, administrative, and professional workers. Use an MNCPPC application with the vacancy announcement number. Applicants must pass a background investigation to be hired. The Employment office will not receive calls.

Maryland State Government

Department of Human Resources
300 West Preston Street
First Floor
Baltimore, MD 21201
(301) 333-7510 (touch-tone)
(301) 333-5044 (rotary)
(800) 492-7845 (inside Maryland)

Although there are state jobs throughout Maryland, there is no state personnel office in the Washington suburban Maryland area. A state job application is required; it must be processed with the vacancy announcement number. A slight hiring preference is given to Maryland residents. No unsolicited applications or résumés are accepted. The Baltimore personnel office is located near the State Center Metro Station. For more information, call (301) 333-0988; call toll-free in Maryland on (800) 332-6347. The TDD number is (301) 225-4006.

Jobs listings may be reviewed at local Job Service offices. They are open from 8:00 a.m.-2:00 p.m. Locations are as follows:

Economic and Employment Development
South Office Building
Wheaton Plaza
Wheaton, MD
(301) 949-5624
or
6321 Greenbelt Road
College Park, MD
(301) 441-2128
or
614 Main Street
Laurel, MD
(301) 206-2020

Marshals' Service, US

see Justice, US Department of

Merit Systems Protection Board

Human Resources Management
1120 Vermont Avenue, NW
Room 850
Washington, DC 20419
(202) 254-8013

MSPB is an independent agency, serving as guardian of the federal merit systems, ensuring protection of federal employees against abuse by agency management. They hire attorneys, administrators, and clerks. The TDD number is (202) 653-8896; the fax number is (202) 653-7130. An SF-171 is required to apply. The headquarters is near McPherson Square and Farragut North Metro Stations. Other jobs are located in Falls Church, VA, and nationally. For more information, call Human Resources at (202) 653-5916.

Minerals Management Service

Department of the Interior
381 Elden Street
Mail Stop 2400
Herndon, VA 22070-4817
(703) 787-1402

MMS regulates national mineral policies and practices, and employs oceanographers, engineers, biologists, chemists, economists, planners, physicists, sociologists, meteorologists, accountants, as well as clerical and support personnel. Jobs are located in Virginia, Washington, DC, and nationally. An SF-171 is required to apply. Call Staffing at (703) 787-1414 or the FTS number at 393-1402. The TDD number is (703) 787-1416.

Mines, Bureau of

Department of the Interior
Division of Personnel
810 7th Street, NW
Washington, DC 20241
(202) 634-4668

The bureau's purpose is twofold. Working with industry and government, they perform research on mining technology in refining metals and making better use of materials. In addition, they gather information, compute statistics, and make presentations worldwide, serving as a resource to other government agencies. An SF-171 is required to apply. They hire engineering, physical science, geology, economics, computer, administration, and clerical workers. Jobs are available in the District and nationally. Headquarters is near the Gallery Place Metro Station. For more information, call (202) 634-4719, or the Department of the Interior Personnel at (202) 208-7150.

Montgomery County

Employment Division
101 Monroe Street, 7th Floor
Rockville, MD 20850
(301) 217-2240 (touch-tone)

x1—how jobs are filled
x2—application information
x8—job listings and clerical testing
x9—for additional information during business hours
x*—back up to previous recording

Montgomery County, MD, is located north of Washington, DC, and southwest of Baltimore. They employ a wide variety of professional, support, and labor positions, including medical, law enforcement, clerical, and human services. Law enforcement officers must be residents of Maryland. The TDD number is (301) 217-1094. The Employment office is near the Rockville Metro Station, and can be reached at (301) 217-2563.

Montgomery County Public Schools

Carver Educational Services Center
850 Hungerford Drive
Rockville, MD 20851
(301) 279-3973

This office maintains the Montgomery County public education system. All vacancies are listed on the jobline, including counselors, maintenance workers, attendants, bus drivers, food service workers, aides, clerks, teachers, and coaches. Some positions require a skills test. The personnel office is near the Rockville Metro Station, and can be reached at (301) 279-3515.

National Aeronautics and Space Administration

Personnel Department
400 Maryland Avenue, SW
Washington, DC 20546
(202) 755-6299

NASA coordinates hiring for management analysts, environmental protection specialists, investigators, auditors, physicists, computer specialists, administrators, and clerks. An SF-171 is required to apply. The positions listed are located at Goddard Space Flight Center, but NASA headquarters is near the L'Enfant Plaza Metro Station. The TDD number is (202) 426-1436; the fax number is (202) 755-4013. For more information and vacancy announcements, call Personnel at (202) 453-8480.

National Association of Securities Dealers

Human Resources
9513 Key West Avenue
Rockville, MD 20850
or

Human Resources
1735 K Street, NW
Washington, DC 20006
(301) 590-0781

NASD is the national federal self-regulatory commission of over-the-counter securities industries. They employ accounting, security, legal, computer, communications, writing, technical, support, and professional workers. The Rockville office is near the Shady Grove Metro Station. The District office is near Farragut North and West Metro Stations. To apply, send a résumé to the office with the specific opening noted. Call Human Resources at (301) 590-6821 or (202) 728-8470.

National Bureau of Standards

see National Institute of Standards and Technology

National Cancer Institute

National Institutes of Health
Personnel Management Branch
Building 31
Room 3-A-34
9000 Rockville Pike
Bethesda, MD 20892
(301) 496-2733

NCI deals with research for diagnosis and treatment of cancer and malignant diseases. They hire professional, scientific, medical, nursing, technical, administrative, and clerical personnel. The Institute is located on the NIH campus near the Medical Center Metro Station. An SF-171 is required. To request a vacancy announcement, leave your name and address and the vacancy announcement number after the jobline message; however, if you live within the Washington metropolitan area, Personnel would prefer that you visit the office to view the announcements. For more information, call Personnel at (301) 496-6862. Clerical applicants should call (301) 402-0092.

National Gallery of Art

Personnel Office
600 Constitution Avenue, NW
Washington, DC 20565
(202) 842-6298

This federal agency collects, displays, and stores all types of art. It receives federal funding for administrative expenses only, while art and exhibits are paid by private donations. They may have openings in clerical, technical, research, retail, historian, librarian, and other museum specialist positions. The museum is near the Judiciary Square Metro Station. An SF-171 is required. For some vacancies, a National Gallery Supplemental Performance Appraisal is also required. Request vacancy announcements at (202) 842-6283. Personnel is open 10:00 a.m.-5:00 p.m., and can be reached at (202) 842-6282.

National Institute of Standards and Technology

US Department of Commerce
Office of Personnel and Civil Rights
Administration Building
Room A-123
Gaithersburg, MD 20899
(703) 538-3344 (touch-tone)
x1—job listings
    x100—executive
    x110—professional engineering and sciences
    x120—technical engineering and sciences
    x130—administrative
    x140—clerical
    x150—trades
x2—how to apply
x3—training information
x4—topical information
x5—additional information

NIST's mission is ". . . to assist industry in the development of technology." They have a modified personnel system that differs from the GS payscale ratings. Instead, NIST uses instead career paths and paybands for most jobs. They hire job categories as listed above. US citizenship and an SF-171 are required. Call Personnel at (301) 975-3007.

National Institutes of Health

Central Employment
9000 Rockville Pike
Building 31, Room BC-315
Bethesda, MD 20892
(301) 496-2403 (touch-tone)
x1—job vacancies
x2—civil service examination
x3—NIH regular summer programs
x4—"stay in school" vacancies
x0—additional information

NIH is a 20-institute medical research and development facility, which also maintains a 600-bed research hospital. This office coordinates entry-level hiring only. Applicants should apply directly to the institute personnel office that has the vacancy. The National Cancer Institute, part of NIH, has a jobline. An SF-171 is required. Most of the institutes are near the Medical Center Metro Station. Central Employment can be reached at (301) 496-2403. The TDD number is (301) 496-7460.

National Park Service

Personnel Office
Department of the Interior
100 Ohio Drive, SW
Room 244
Washington, DC 20242
(202) 619-7111

This federal office operates the National Capital region's parks. Job opportunities may include security, gardening, maintenance, clerical, labor, biology, ranger, driver, accounting, and service. Jobs are located in Washington, DC, Virginia, Maryland, and the eastern panhandle of West Virginia. An SF-171 is required. The TDD number is (202) 619-7364. To request a job description, leave your name and address and the job announcement number after the jobline tone. For more information, call personnel at (202) 619-7256.

National Security Agency

Attention: M-323
Fort Meade, MD 20755-6000

NSA is an intelligence installation, supplying information to the government. They hire degreed math, computer, electrical engineering, and languages professionals, as well as clerical and administrative workers. A security clearance and US citizenship are required. An SF-171 is required to apply. For more information, call Employment at (301) 859-6444.

National Technical Information Service

Department of Commerce
Personnel Operations
5285 Port Royal Road
Springfield, VA 22161
(703) 487-4680 (touch-tone)
x1, then x1, then x2

NTIS is an agency providing technical information to other government offices. They offer flex-time to their employees. Job openings are primarily in clerical fields, but limited opportunities may exist in warehouse, marketing, and technical specialist areas. An SF-171 is required to apply. For more information, call Personnel at (703) 487-4680, x1, then x2.

Naval Academy, US

Civilian Personnel Department
Stop 20-B
Halligan Hall
181 Wainwright Road
Annapolis, MD 21402-5009
(301) 267-3821

USNA is the college-level education and training facility for US Navy officers. Civilian employment opportunities often include security, maintenance, accounting, mechanical, supervisory, engineering, clerical, support, shipfitting, and educational positions. An SF-171 and security clearance are required. For more information, call Personnel at (301) 267-3822 or (301) 267-3388.

Naval Air Station, Patuxent River

Civilian Personnel Department
Building 463
Patuxent River, MD 20670-5409
(301) 863-4801

This is a US Navy installation in Saint Mary's County, MD, on the Chesapeake Bay. They also service the Naval Electronic Systems Engineering Activity in Saint Inigoes, MD. The jobline may advertise professional, clerical, law enforcement, nursing, computer, engineering, technical, and aviation vacancies. An SF-171 and security clearance are required. For more information, call Personnel at (301) 863-3746. The TDD number is (301) 863-3545.

Northern Virginia Community College

Human Resources Office
4001 Wakefield Chapel Road
Room 203
Annandale, VA 22003
(703) 323-3444 (touch-tone)
x111—full-time faculty and administration
x333—part-time/adjunct teaching positions
x444—full-time staff
x555—part-time staff
x666—hourly wage positions

NVCC offers community college education at the Alexandria, Manassas, Woodbridge, Loudoun (Sterling), and Annandale campuses. They accept résumés or Commonwealth of Virginia applications for faculty, part-time teaching, administrative, clerical, maintenance, computer, accounting, security, library, lab assistant, and service positions. Human Resources keeps applications on file for two years. To activate an application for non-faculty positions, call (703) 323-3021 or (703) 323-3124. To activate a faculty application, call (703) 323-3335. For more information, call Human Resources at (703) 323-3110.

Northern Virginia Training Center

Personnel Department
9901 Braddock Road
Fairfax, VA 22032
(703) 323-2804

NVTC is a residential treatment facility (500 staff, 250 residents) for individuals with mental retardation. They employ clinical, direct care, clerical, support, management, nursing, warehouse, and maintenance staff. A Commonwealth of Virginia application is required together with notation on the position title, number, and closing date. For more information, call Personnel at (703) 323-4012. The main switchboard TDD number is (703) 323-4001.

Overseas Private Investment Corporation

Human Resources
1615 M Street, NW
Washington, DC 20527
(202) 457-7013

OPIC is a small federal agency that encourages the economic growth of developing third world countries by providing loans and political risk insurance to private investors. Employment opportunities may include financial managers, loan officers, and clerical positions. The office is located near the Farragut North Metro Station. An SF-171, proof of US citizenship, and security clearance are required. For more information, call Human Resources at (202) 457-7075 or leave a message after the jobline tone. For the intern program, call (202) 457-7094.

Patent and Trademark Office

US Department of Commerce
Office of Personnel
C & E Division, Suite 700
PO Box 171
Washington, DC 20231
or

2011 Crystal Drive
Suite 700, Crystal Park I
Arlington, VA 22202
(703) 557-0297 (touch-tone)
x230—job listings

PTO is the national register of inventions and trademarks. They employ
clerks, examiners, and other professionals. The main office is near the Crystal
City Metro Station. An SF-171 is required. For more information, call Personnel at (703) 557-3631 or (800) 327-2909.

Peace Corps

Personnel
1990 K Street, NW
Seventh Floor
Washington, DC 20526
(202) 775-2214

This is the federal international outreach agency. The jobline lists staff, not
volunteer, positions. They are organized on an FP (Foreign Service Peace
Corps) payscale; employment is only for 30-month appointments. Paid positions include communications, medical, administrative, computer, financial, supervisory, agriculture, vocational, and clerical. The Personnel office
coordinates local hiring as well. The office is near the Farragut West Metro
Station. An SF-171 is required to apply. Call Personnel at (202) 606-3400
to request a vacancy announcement.

Postal Service, US

Headquarters Personnel Division
Room 1813
475 L'Enfant Plaza, SW
Washington, DC 20260-4261
(202) 268-3218 (touch-tone)
x1—technical, professional, managerial
x2—clerical exams and vacancies
x3—custodial
x4—maintenance

The US Postal Service coordinates the country's mail. Different departments
include special and overnight delivery. Technical, professional, and managerial applicants must complete SF-171, Form 2591, and résumé with salary
history. Send these forms to the appropriate Team designated on the jobline.
Custodial applicants must apply in person, complete an SF-171 and Form
2479, and then pass the custodial exam. Headquarters is near the L'Enfant

Plaza Metro Station. For more information, call Personnel at (202) 268-3646.

Prince George's County

Personnel
Largo Government Center
9201 Basil Court, #200
Landover, MD 20785
(301) 952-3408

PG County is located in Maryland, east and south of Washington, bordering Montgomery County and the Potomac River. The jobline may include engineering, maintenance, law enforcement, firefighting, corrections, library, social service, planning, and clerical announcements. Some hiring preference is given to county residents. Applicants must use the county's application; some positions require testing. They accept no unsolicited résumés or applications. For more information, call Police recruiting at (301) 808-1800, Firefighter recruiting at (301) 808-1791, or Personnel at (301) 925-5330. The TDD number is (301) 925-5207.

Prince George's County Public Schools

Instructional Personnel
14201 School Lane, Room 131
Upper Marlboro, MD 20772-9983

This is the nation's 17th largest school district. Personnel advertises job vacancies in the *Washington Post*, and circulates listings in every school office. A county school application is required, as are transcripts, teaching certificate, and National Teachers' Examination results (as applicable), references, and application addenda. For more information and to request an application, call the Application Center at (301) 952-6180 or (800) 486-2673.

Prince William County

Personnel
4343 Ridgewood Center Drive
Woodbridge, VA 22192
(703) 792-6645
(703) 631-1703 (metro number)

PW County is located in Virginia, south of Washington, DC, and Fairfax County. They have a wide variety of employment opportunities, including bindery, social service, engineering, firefighting, collections, courier, accounting, management, maintenance, support, planning, communications, law enforcement, and library work. To apply, use a county application, writing the vacancy announcement number and title on each. For more information, call Personnel at (703) 792-6640 or (703) 631-1703, local to northern Virginia. The TDD number is (703) 792-6291.

Prince William County Public Schools

Classified Personnel
14800 Joplin Road
Manassas, VA 22110
(703) 791-2776 (touch-tone)
x2—job listings
x4—teacher transfer opportunities

This office coordinates the classified (nonteaching) hiring for Prince William public schools. Job opportunities may include maintenance, clerical, service, bookkeeping, and administrative support. Call (703) 791-8734 to request a county application; the application must be completed using the position number. For jobs with the bus department, call (703) 368-0176. Clerical positions require testing. For more information, call Personnel at (703) 791-8733.

Public Debt, Bureau of the

Department of the Treasury
Employment Branch, Department V
300 13th Street, SW
Room 223
Washington, DC 20239-1400
(202) 447-1407

This bureau handles savings bonds and treasury bills, notes, and bonds. The jobline lists clerical, computer, accounting, support, security, and supervisory vacancies. The office is near the Smithsonian Metro Station. An SF-171 is required. The TDD number is (202) 447-0950. Call Employment at (202) 447-9798.

Public Health Service

Office of the Assistant Secretary for Health
Department of Health and Human Services
Personnel
17-A-07 Parklawn Building
5600 Fisher's Lane
Rockville, MD 20857
(301) 443-1986

PHS regulates the public health service system. The office does not provide medical treatment. This personnel offices also services the Agency for Health Care Policy and Research in Rockville. They employ clerical, accounting, computer, contracting, and supervisory personnel. They also have positions for space managers and medical staff. Jobs are located in Washington, DC, and Bethesda, and in the Rockville office near the Twinbrook Metro Station. An SF-171 and performance appraisal are required to apply. For more information, call Personnel at (301) 443-6900. The TDD number is (301) 443-3931.

Resolution Trust Corporation

see Federal Deposit Insurance Corporation

Senate Placement Office

Hart Senate Office Building
Room 142-B
Washington, DC 20510

The Senate Placement Office refers résumés of applicants to Senators, Senate personal staff, and Committee offices. Available jobs may include legislative assistant, legislative aide, legislative correspondent, office manager, mail clerk, staff assistant, or other clerical positions. When vacancies occur, the Placement office is contacted for a list of appropriate applicants. The senator's office will then contact the applicants they wish to interview. The Placement Office also displays a job vacancy listing. US citizenship is required, except for citizens of some countries with whom Congress has an agreement to exchange workers.

Apply in person to provide a copy of your résumé, complete an application (not an SF-171), take a typing test, and attend an informational interview. The office holds interviews on a walk-in basis, from 10:00 a.m.-noon and 1:00 p.m.-3:00 p.m. Monday-Thursday, and 10:00 a.m.-noon and 1:00 p.m.-2:00 p.m. Fridays. They hold applications for 1 month. The office is near the Union Street Metro Station. Call the staff at (202) 224-9167; the TDD number is (202) 224-4215.

Small Business Administration

1111 18th Street, NW
4th & 6th Floors
or
PO Box 19993
Washington, DC 20036
(202) 634-4950 (touch-tone)
(800) 827-5722 (touch-tone)

x1—main directory, programs list
   x1—employee directory
   x2—general information
   x3—business assistance programs and counseling services
   x4—Affirmative Action programs
   x5—loan and financial information
   x6—address and directions
   x7—legal and licensure information

SBA is not a clearinghouse for employment; however, they offer services listed above to assist individuals wanting to initiate their own small businesses. They are located near the Farragut North and West Metro Stations. The hotline is only operational during business hours.

Smithsonian Institution, The

Employment Office
900 Jefferson Drive, SW
Washington, DC 20560
(202) 287-3102 (touch-tone)
x8—application information
x9—request vacancy announcement
x1—federal job listings
x2—trust fund listings (privately funded)
    x3—wage grade
    x4—guard, museum security
    x5—clerical (some jobs have special pay provisions)
    x6—technical, administrative support
    x7—professional GS 5-15
    x8—senior level
    x*—repeat message

The Smithsonian Institution is the national museum foundation with over ten museums in Washington, DC. They employ federal and nonfederal workers. Possible openings include maintenance, security, historian, technician, clerk, accounting, computer, support, writing, transportation, communications, education, chemistry, photography, warehouse, service, buyers, and library vacancies. Jobs are located in Washington, DC, and Maryland, and require an SF-171 for all vacancies (federal and nonfederal). A Supplemental Sheet is required for some openings. The Employment Office is near the Smithsonian Metro Station, and can be reached at (202) 287-3100. The TDD number is (202) 287-3498.

Social Security Administration

see Federal Job Information Center

State, Department of

Office of Civil Service Recruiting
Staffing Services
2201 C Street, NW
Room 2819
or
PO Box 18657
Washington, DC 20036-8657
(202) 647-7284

The State Department is the office coordinating all foreign relations. All jobs advertised require Civil Service status to apply, unless otherwise noted. Openings may include medical, technical, foreign affairs, transportation, administration, operations research, construction, maintenance, personal services, interior design, inspection, accounting, security, and programming. An SF-171, SF-50, performance appraisal, drug screen, and security clearance are required. For more information or to request a vacancy announcement, call (202) 647-6132.

Supreme Court of the US

Personnel Office
1 First Street, NE
Room 3
Washington, DC 20543

This office does not have a jobline but keeps desirable SF-171 applications on file for one year. Their hiring includes assistant clerk, new case analyst, budget accounting assistant, and police officer (ongoing). The office is near the Capitol South Metro Station. For more information, call (202) 479-3404.

Transportation, US Department of

Central Employment
400 7th Street, SW
Washington, DC 20590
(202) 366-9397 (touch-tone)

x1—job listings
x3—clerical testing
x4—student programs
x5—personnel offices within the department
x6—job fairs

Offices at this location include the Office of the Secretary, Federal Highway Administration, National Highway Traffic Safety Board, Urban Mass Transportation, Maritime Administration, Research and Special Programs, Inspector General, and Federal Railroad Office. Also in this department, but at a different site, are the Coast Guard, (202) 267-2331; Federal Aviation Administration, (202) 267-8007 (see also jobline); and Federal Land and Sea Office, (315) 764-3200. An SF-171 is required. Central Employment is open 7:00 a.m.-6:00 p.m. There is an application dropbox for after business hours. For more information, call Personnel at (202) 366-9397, x0. The TDD number is (202) 366-3760.

Treasury, US Department of

Bureau of Departmental Offices
Personnel
15th Street and Pennsylvania Avenue, NW
Room 1318
Washington, DC 20220
(202) 566-2540

The Treasury Department handles the country's currency. The Bureau of Departmental Offices is only one of 13 within this department. An SF-171 is required to apply. They hire economists, accountants, proofreaders, administrative staff, and maintenance workers. The main office is located beside the White House near the McPherson Square Metro Station. For more information or vacancy announcement request, call Personnel at (202) 566-5411, which is also TDD accessible.

US Postal Service

see Postal Service, US

Veterans' Administration Medical Center

Personnel Services
50 Irving Street, NW
Room 1-121
Washington, DC 20422
(202) 745-8000 (touch-tone)
x1, then x4, then x1
  x1—nursing jobs
  x2—all others

The Center's jobline is active only in the evenings. During business hours, ask for personnel. Jobs advertised are for the hospital; they include clinical, technical, security, nursing, administration, clerical, maintenance, and service. An SF-171 is required to apply. For more information, call (202) 745-8204. Call the nursing recruiter at (202) 745-8477.

Virginia, Commonwealth of

Employment Commission
386 South Pickett Street
Alexandria, VA
(703) 823-4139
or
8000 Lee Highway
Falls Church, VA
(703) 573-5045
or
8675 Phoenix Drive
Manassas, VA
(703) 361-1126
or
152 Enterprise Street
Sterling, VA
(703) 444-2300

Virginia lists job vacancies through the Job Service in the above offices. All vacancies are printed on microfiche and must be viewed at the Job Service. Commonwealth of Virginia applications are accepted for vacancies only, but some individual offices may review résumés and request special attention to applications.

Voice of America

Office of Personnel
Room 1543
330 Independence Avenue, SW
Washington, DC 20547
(202) 619-0909

This federal office coordinates American shortwave radio broadcasting in 43 languages around the world. They have clerical, engineering, computer, and broadcasting job openings, especially for those fluent in languages other than English. Jobs are located in Washington, DC, and around the world. An SF-171 is required. The Personnel office is near the Federal Center SW Metro Station, and can be reached at (202) 619-3117.

Washington Convention Center

Human Resources
900 9th Street, NW
Washington, DC 20001
(202) 371-4498

This is the major convention and meeting forum in Washington, DC. They regularly hire security, clerical, journeyman maintenance, engineering, convention planning, and supervisory workers. Apply in person Monday, Tuesday, and Friday, 9:00 a.m.-2:00 p.m. at 11th Street and New York Avenue, NW. The Center is near Metro Center Metro Station. For more information or to request an application, call Employment at (202) 371-3089 or wait after the jobline for an operator.

Washington, DC Government and Public Schools

see District of Columbia Government
see District of Columbia Public Schools

Washington Navy Yard

Department of the Navy
Consolidated Civilian Personnel Office
Building 200
Washington, DC 20374-2000
(202) 433-4930

This CCPO, located at the Washington Navy Yard, coordinates employment for clinical, computer, accounting, support, security, supervisory, astronomy, social service, firefighting, editing, writing, communications, engineering, labor, warehouse, logistics, and others. See also the CCPO in Crystal City. Jobs are in Washington, DC, Virginia, and Maryland. An SF-171 is required to apply. The Personnel office is near the Eastern Market Metro Station. They can be reached at (202) 433-4931.

Appendix C
PRIVATE SECTOR JOBLINES

This appendix is a directory of employers using jobline telephone numbers. Employers are listed alphabetically with the address, jobline number, and a short description of the business. Common acronyms are also provided for reference. Some employers listed do not use joblines, but they are included here because they have regular openings.

Ameribanc Savings Bank

Human Resources
7630 Little River Turnpike
Annandale, VA 22003
(703) 658-5627

This bank provides competitive, comprehensive, banking services. They employ tellers, clerks, customer service representatives, proofreaders, collectors, accountants, and administrators. Jobs are located throughout northern Virginia. Applications are taken Monday-Friday, 8:30 a.m.-1:00 p.m. Human Resources can be contacted directly at (703) 658-1015.

American Medical Laboratories, Inc.

Human Resources Department
11091 Main Street
Fairfax, VA 22030
(703) 385-4905 (touch-tone)
x1—nontechnical
x2—technical

These facilities perform clinical testing for health care providers. They employ medical and lab technologists, aides, histotechnologists, and clerical personnel. Headquarters is located in Fairfax; there are satellite labs in other locations. For more information, call Human Resources at (703) 385-4830.

American Society for Training and Development

4227 46th Street, NW
Washington, DC 20016

The Washington Metropolitan chapter of ASTD serves to coordinate related job openings for human resources/personnel professionals at all levels. They list both public and private employers. One must be a member of ASTD, however, to access their joblines. To join, call (202) 362-1498 or (301) 340-7493.

American Telephone and Telegraph

Personnel Office
3033 Chain Bridge Road, Room L-108
Oakton, VA 22185
(800) 545-9568 (touch-tone)
x1—job listings
x2—directions to office

AT&T is a national telephone long-distance utility company. The joblines contain application information for entry-level account representatives, sales, clerical, and technical positions only. The office coordinates hiring for Virginia, Maryland, Washington, DC, and West Virginia. For management openings, call (201) 898-8210. AT&T employees can call (201) 898-3995 for advancement opportunities. For more information, call Personnel at (703) 691-6952.

American University

Personnel Services
Cassell Center
4451 Massachusetts Avenue, NW
Room 204
Washington, DC 20016
or
Employment Services
Cassell Center
Box 281 Eagle Station
Washington, DC 20016-8055
(202) 885-2639 (touch-tone)

x1—new job listings
x2—previous job listings
x3—salary information
x4—employment procedures

AU is a private academic institution educating in all disciplines. Occupations listed on the jobline include all staff, professional, support and labor personnel, except for teaching, food service, and housekeeping. Apply in person or send a résumé. For food service, call Marriott at (202) 885-3175; for housekeeping, call Service Master at (202) 885-2355. For more information, call Employment Services at (202) 885-2591.

Amtrak Corporate Office

Human Resources Department
60 Massachusetts Avenue, NE
Washington, DC 20002
(202) 906-3866
or
Amtrak
Division Personnel Services
900 2nd Street, NE
Lower Level
Washington, DC 20002

Amtrak is a national rail passenger corporation, employing management, technical, support, and onboard workers. For management (professional) jobs, send résumé to Human Resources. For train and support jobs, send your résumé or apply in person at Division Personnel near the Union Station Metro Station. For more information, call Corporate Human Resources at (202) 906-2399.

Arbitron Ratings

Human Resources
4320 Ammendale Road
Beltsville, MD 20705
(301) 497-5099

Arbitron is a business for collecting and analyzing national television ratings information. The jobline advertises clerical and data-entry positions only. The jobline machine is active only when positions are open. The clerical jobs are located in Beltsville, MD, although there are other offices with statistical and administrative functions. Walk-in interview times are noted on the recording. For more information, call Human Resources at (301) 497-3812.

Atlantic Research Corporation

Aerospace Group
Employment
5945 Wellington Road
Gainesville, VA 22065
or
Professional Services Group
Human Resources Employment
1375 Piccard Drive
Rockville, MD 20850
(703) 642-6411

ARC is a high-tech firm with two groups: aerospace, for solid rocket motor design and manufacture, and Professional Services, for government engineering contracts. Locally, jobs are in Gainesville, Orange, and Alexandria, VA. ARC also offers national opportunities. Their jobline includes administrative, clerical, safety, contracts, finance, engineering, support, and professional positions. Most of the jobs require a security clearance. Call Human Resources at (703) 642-6300 or (800) 843-6510. The fax number is (703) 642-6496.

Bell Atlantic Network Services

see Chesapeake and Potomac Telephone

Blue Cross/Blue Shield of the National Capital Area

Human Resources
550 12th Street, SW
Washington, DC 20065
(202) 479-7470

Blue Cross/Blue Shield is a recognized leader in the health insurance industry. They hire accountants, actuaries, computer professionals, nurses, customer service representatives, and administrators. CapitalCare health maintenance organization is a subsidiary of the system. The main office is near the L'Enfant Plaza Metro Station and can be reached by leaving a message after the jobline tone. The TDD number is (202) 479-7673.

Bridgestone/Firestone

(800) 832-4536

Bridgestone and Firestone screen automotive technicians through their 24-hour jobline. To apply, leave a message for the recruiter by stating your name, telephone number, geographical work area desired (all areas of Washington, Baltimore, Maryland, and Virginia are represented), and summary of related experience. Applicants may also file a job application at any Bridgestone or Firestone store.

Cable News Network

Washington Bureau
820 First Street, NE
Washington, DC 20002
(202) 898-7900, ask for jobline
(operational during business hours only)

CNN broadcasts news 24 hours a day. Send a résumé for their review. They promote from within. The office is located near the Union Station Metro Station and does not accept telephone calls.

Cable TV Montgomery

Human Resources
20 West Gude Drive
Rockville, MD 20850
(301) 294-7679

Cable TV Montgomery provide cable television service to Montgomery County, MD. They may have openings in collections, customer service, sales, installation, administration, or technical work. Send a résumé or apply in person. Call the office at (301) 294-7600. The TDD number is (301) 294-7686.

CapitalCare

Human Resources Department
1921 Gallows Road
Ninth Floor
Vienna, VA 22182
(703) 761-5411 (touch-tone)

CapitalCare is a health maintenance organization; medical care is provided by participating physicians in Virginia. They are a subsidiary of Blue Cross/Blue Shield. They may have jobs in claims analysis, customer service (members, doctors, hospitals), clerical, utilization review nurses, marketing, sales, and administration. Send your résumé to apply. For more information on contacting Human Resources, follow jobline instructions.

Catholic University of America

Personnel
Administration Building
620 Michigan Avenue, NE
Washington, DC 20064
(202) 319-5263

Catholic University is a large, private Catholic institution. Its jobline may advertise administrative, computer, clerical, maintenance, library, faculty, and service positions. Write down the job order number for inquiry and application. All jobs are on campus near the Brookland Metro Station. Call Personnel at (202) 319-5050 for more information.

Center for Naval Analyses

Human Resources
4401 Ford Avenue
Alexandria, VA 22302-0268
(703) 824-2999

CNA is a federally funded research and development center (FFRDC), working primarily for the Navy and the Marines. They study a range of military subjects from weapons systems to recruitment and training. A security clearance and US Citizenship are required for employment. CNA hires support and administrative staff, and research, high-tech, and analysis professionals to the doctoral level. CNA also offers tuition assistance and a shuttle to the Pentagon Metro Station 7:30 a.m.-6:00 p.m. Call Personnel at (703) 824-2047.

Chesapeake and Potomac Telephone

Employment
2980 Fairview Park Drive
First Floor
Falls Church, VA 22042
(703) 204-7201
or
Employment
1738 Elton Road
Silver Spring, MD 20903
(301) 454-0754
or

Employment
930 H Street, NW
Washington, DC 20001
(202) 347-7070
(800) 633-4747

C&P is a local- and long-distance telephone utility company serving the US East Coast. These offices include hiring for Bell Atlantic Network Services. C&P accepts applications and résumés for job openings only. For more information, call the Employment offices: Virginia at (703) 204-7200, Maryland at (301) 454-0755, and the District at (202) 392-3609. The District's office is near Gallery Place and Metro Center Metro Stations.

Children's Hospital National Medical Center

Human Resources
111 Michigan Avenue, NW
Washington, DC 20010
(202) 745-2060

Children's Hospital is a nationally renowned medical facility with clinics in Washington, DC, Silver Spring, MD, Gaithersburg, MD, and Fairfax, VA. They have a wide variety of employment opportunities in clinical, support, and labor positions. The TDD number is (202) 745-3444. For Human Resources, call (202) 745-2080; for the nursing recruiter, call (202) 745-5396.

Clement Associates

see ICF International, Inc.

Discovery Channel

Human Resources
7700 Wisconsin Avenue
Bethesda, MD 20814-3522
(301) 986-0444 (touch-tone)
x87—job information

The Discovery Channel programs scientific, technical, and documentary entertainment for cable television. They prefer applicants to send in résumés with cover letters stating employment objectives. They will then review the résumés for 4-6 weeks. The office is near the Bethesda Metro Station. To request more information, leave a message at the end of the employment recording.

District Photo, Inc.

Personnel Department
10619 Baltimore Avenue
Beltsville, MD 20705
(301) 937-5627

District Photo is a photo-finishing plant open 24 hours a day. The jobline advertises production, customer service representative, security, technical and management opportunities. Walk-in interviews are conducted Monday - Friday, 8 a.m.-5 p.m. Applicants must bring proof of the right to work in the United States with a valid driver's license and a Social Security card, birth certificate, or employment authorization (green card). The TDD number is (301) 595-3749. Call Personnel at (301) 937-5300, x220.

Doctors' Community Hospital

Human Resources
8118 Good Luck Road, #402
Lanham, MD 20706
(301) 552-8000
x1—job listings
x2—general information
x3—benefit information
x0—operator

Doctors' Community Hospital is located in Prince George's County. They employ administrative and clerical staff, medical technical specialists, nurses of all specialties, and other medical support staff. It is also home of the Maryland Blood Center. Applications are accepted Monday-Friday from 9:00 a.m. to 3:00 p.m. The TDD number is (301) 552-8078; Human Resources can be reached at (301) 552-8080. The fax number is (301) 552-9306.

Eastman Kodak

Attention: Personnel Relations
1100 North Glebe Road
Arlington, VA 22201
(716) 724-4609 (touch-tone)
x1—job listings

This diverse manufacturing and service company deals with information systems, computers, copiers, technical systems, life sciences, chemicals, photographic equipment, and the Sterling Drug Co. Jobs are located nationally and locally near the Ballston Metro Station. Some jobs require a security clearance. Applicants may apply in person or send a résumé. Call local personnel at (703) 908-5567.

Fairfax Hospital

Employment Office
3300 Gallows Road
Falls Church, VA 22046
(703) 698-2374

This 656-bed acute care teaching hospital employs support, labor, professional, and clinical personnel. Nursing and physician vacancies are not on the Dial-A-Job. Call Employment at (703) 698-3156 for more information.

Fairfax Nursing Center

Personnel
10701 Main Street
Fairfax, VA 22030
(703) 385-0013

This is a family-owned 200-bed skilled nursing home. Their jobline advertises nursing, clerical, maintenance, and administrative positions. Applications are accepted Monday-Wednesday, 10 a.m.-2:00 p.m., or by appointment. For more information, request Personnel at (703) 273-7705. The fax number is (703) 273-8077.

Federal Home Loan Mortgage Corporation

Human Resources
8200 Jones Branch Drive
Mail Stop HR/120
McLean, VA 22102
(703) 903-2970 (touch-tone)

x1—address
x2—information
x3—clerical, administrative, accounting
x4—financial analysis
x5—legal, risk management, finance
x6—sales, advertising, public relations, personnel
x7—computer systems professionals

Freddie Mac is a stockholder corporation created by Congress to ensure the continuation of funds in support of affordable home ownership and rental housing. They deal with the secondary mortgage market, buying mortgages from lenders and selling securities to investors. They employ personnel as listed above. Jobs are located in McLean, Reston, and Arlington (Crystal City), VA; in Washington, DC; and in New York City (the legal office). The McLean office is next to Unisys, which operates a free shuttle to metrorail. To apply, send your résumé to the address provided for the desired job. Call (703) 903-2860 for Employment Services.

Federal National Mortgage Association

Employment Hotline
3900 Wisconsin Avenue, NW
Washington, DC 20016
(202) 752-5300 (touch-tone)

x1—clerical
x2—computer
x3—finance, accounting
x4—legal
x5—marketing

x6—policy
x7—other programs
x8—regional
x9—beginning
x11—repeat sequence

Fannie Mae, the country's housing partner, is a congressionally chartered, shareholder-owned company and the nation's largest investor in home mortgages. The office hires the occupational categories listed above, and is located near the Tenleytown Metro Station. Record the job requisition number and title from the jobline; include this information on the heading of your cover letter and forward with your résumé. Call Human Resources at (202) 752-7630.

First Advantage Mortgage Corporation

Human Resources
8401 Colesville Road
Seventh Floor
Silver Spring, MD 20910
(800) 477-4473 (touch-tone)

x6—general information
   x1—job listings
   x2—how to apply
   x3—location
   x4—additional information
   x8—return to main menu

First Advantage is the local mortgage firm of First American Bankshares. The main office is in Columbia, MD, but Human Resources is near the Silver Spring Metro Station. They may have realtor representative, customer service, accountant, or clerk jobs available. Apply in person or send résumé. For more information, call Human Resources at (301) 565-7100.

First American Bank

Human Resources
8401 Colesville Road
Seventh Floor
Silver Spring, MD 20910
or

Human Resources
1715 Pinnacle Drive
Fourth Floor
McLean, VA 22102
or
Human Resources
740 15th Street, NW
Washington, DC 20005
(800) 477-4473 (touch-tone)
x3—Maryland general information
x1, then x2—Virginia general information
x2—Washington general information
  x1—job listings
  x2—how to apply
  x3—locations
  x4—additional information
  x8—return to main menu

First American Bank is part of First American, the largest bank headquartered in the Washington area with 180 local branches. They hire personnel in customer service, maintenance, teller, administrative, security, operations coordinator, corporate services, corporate relations, loan reviewer, and mail clerk. Apply 9:00 a.m.-4:00 p.m., or send your résumé. The Maryland office is near the Silver Spring Metro Station and can be reached at (301) 565-7100. The Virginia Human Resources can be reached at (703) 760-6700. The Washington office is near the McPherson Square Metro Station and can be reached at (202) 637-6317.

First American Reston Operations Center

Metro Corporate
1880 Campus Commons Drive
Reston, VA 22091
(800) 477-4473 (touch-tone)
x1, then x1—general information
x1—job listings
x2—how to apply
x3—locations
x4—additional information
x8—return to main menu

This office processes checks, bank statements, and mail for all branches of First American Bank. It may have openings in mail, accounting, clerical, or proofreading. Apply by calling for an appointment or send your résumé. For more information, call (703) 648-2848.

First American Staff Temporaries, Inc.

1751 Pinnacle Drive
Fourth Floor
McLean, VA 22102
or
1880 Campus Commons Drive
Second Floor
Reston, VA 22091
or
8401 Colesville Road
Seventh Floor
Silver Spring, MD 20910
(800) 477-4473 (touch-tone)
x5—general information
    x1—job listings
    x2—how to apply
    x3—locations
    x4—additional information
    x8—return to main menu

These offices provide clerical and customer service temporary staff for First American Bank throughout the Washington metropolitan area. Positions may include clerk, secretary, word processor, and typist. Knowledge of Word Perfect, Lotus, VAX 2020 is desirable. Apply by appointment only. Call the McLean (Tyson's Corner) office at (703) 760-6343, the Reston office at (703) 648-3520, and the Silver Spring office (near the Silver Spring Metro Station) at (301) 565-7015.

Future Aviation Professionals of America

Human Resources
4959 Massachusetts Boulevard
Atlanta, GA 30337

FAPA researches pilot, mechanic, and flight attendant jobs, and they provide monthly national job listings and related information to members only. Pilots and mechanics must be licensed to join. Flight attendants need have no previous qualifications. Call (800) 538-5627, x184, or (404) 997-8097 to subscribe. The fax number is (404) 997-8111.

Gallaudet University

Human Resources
800 Florida Avenue, NE
Chapel Hall
Washington, DC 20002
(202) 651-5358 (auditory, touch-tone)
(202) 651-5359 (TDD)

x1—American Sign Language   x4—professional
     requirement explained   x5—faculty
x2—secretarial   x6—application information
x3—technical, service   x7—repeat sequence

Gallaudet is ". . . a multi-purpose educational institution and resource center serving people with hearing impairments, around the world, through a full range of academic, research, and public service programs." The joblines include jobs designated by the extensions above; however, they do not include food service. Human Resources is open 8:30 a.m.-4:00 p.m., and can be reached at (202) 651-5352, which is also TDD accessible.

Gannett Company, Inc.

Employee Relations
1100 Wilson Boulevard
Arlington, VA 22234
(703) 284-6054 (touch-tone)

Gannett (pronounced, gan NET) is a multimedia corporation in television, radio, and newspapers. The corporate headquarters in Rosslyn provides the business support for the national company. It is near the Rosslyn Metro Station; some jobs may also be located in the Silver Spring, MD, Operations Center. Jobs that may be available include administration, clerical, financial, computer, and business. To apply, mail or fax your résumé at (703) 558-4697. Employee Relations plans to have a national jobline, which will include journalism, advertising, and technical positions. They prefer not to receive any telephone inquiries.

Georgetown University

Human Resources
Healy Building
37th and O Streets, NW
Washington, DC 20057
(202) 687-2521

Georgetown is ". . . dedicated to researching, implementing, and teaching. It is the oldest Catholic university, celebrating its bicentennial anniversary in 1989." It employs clerical, dental, medical, support, library, technical, clinical, scientific, research, accounting, security, insurance, administrative, and professional personnel. There are satellite locations in Rockville, Gaithersburg, and in the District at 2nd and F Streets, NW. The Law Center is near the Judiciary Square Metro Station. The hospital has its own jobline listed below. Apply in person for specific vacancies. For more information, call Personnel at (202) 687-2500.

Georgetown University Hospital

Human Resources Department
2233 Wisconsin Avenue, NW
Suite 318
Washington, DC 20007
(202) 784-2683

GUH is a nationally known medical facility employing clinical, technical, administrative, support, computer, security, and nursing personnel. Send a résumé or apply in person for specific vacancies. Nurses can call the recruiter at (202) 784-2370 or (800) 323-9904. Call Human Resources at (202) 784-2660.

Giant Food

Main Employment Office
6300 Sheriff Road
Landover, MD 20785
(301) 341-8531 (Maryland and Washington jobs)
(301) 341-8532 (Virginia jobs)

Giant is a full-service food store chain with a tremendous amount of employment opportunities. The joblines list instructions for applying for part-time entry-level food service, clerical, labor, and cashier positions. Giant also has a managerial career development program. Listen to the joblines for Mobile Employment Center locations or apply at the office 9:00 a.m.-4:00 p.m. The TDD number is (301) 341-4327; the office can be reached directly at (301) 341-4382. Applications are also accepted at:

Giant Employment Office
7528 Annapolis Road
Lanham, MD 20784
(301) 577-7456

This office is located near the New Carrollton Metro Station. It is open Monday, Wednesday, and Friday, 9:00 a.m.-noon.

Giant Employment Office
12085 Rockville Pike
Rockville, MD 20852
(301) 881-5782

This office is open Monday, Tuesday, Wednesday, and Friday 9:00 a.m.-4:30 p.m., and Thursday 9:00-8:00 p.m. It is near the Twinbrook Metro Station.

Giant Employment Office
6300-B Springfield Plaza
Old Keene Mill and Backlick Roads
Springfield, VA 22150
(703) 569-4630

This office is open Monday-Friday, 9:00 a.m.-4:30 p.m.

Giant Employment Office
9452 Main Street
Fairfax, VA 22031
(703) 425-4820

This office is open Monday, Tuesday, Wednesday, and Friday, 9:00 a.m.-5:00 p.m., and Thursday 9:00 a.m.-8:00 p.m.

Greater Laurel-Beltsville Hospital

Human Resources
7100 Contee Road
Laurel, MD 20707
(301) 497-7909

The jobline includes openings at the Laurel facility, a 280-bed general hospital, and the Bowie Health Center. It advertises openings in nursing, clinical, technical, professional, clerical, administrative, service, labor, and support occupations. For more information, call Human Resources at (301) 497-7905.

Greater Southeast Community Hospital

Employment
1310 Southern Avenue, SE
Washington, DC 20032
(202) 574-6983

GSECH is a medical facility located in southeast Washington, DC. Their jobline includes vacancies at the Fort Washington Ambulatory Care Center. Jobs often open are clinical, professional, technical, maintenance, administrative, and clerical. Nurses and other allied health professionals can call the

Recruiter in Employment at (202) 574-6911. All other others apply in person, 8:00 a.m.-noon.

Group Health Association

Human Resources Department
4301 Connecticut Avenue, NW
Washington, DC 20008
(202) 364-2080 (touch-tone)

This health maintenance organization serves more than 100,000 members in branches throughout the metropolitan area. Job openings may include nurses, support and clerical workers, technicians, pharmacists, risk managers, computer professionals, and marketing representatives. Apply in person on Tuesdays and Thursdays 9:00 a.m.-3:00 p.m., or send a résumé. Human Resources is near the Van Ness/UDC Metro Station, and can be reached at (202) 364-2022.

GTE Government Systems

Staffing Department
15000 Conference Center Drive
Chantilly, VA 22021-3808
(703) 818-5627

GTE is a national telecommunications company, which recently merged with Contel Federal Systems, hiring computer information systems, engineering, and other high-tech professionals, as well as administrative support workers. They have offices in Chantilly, VA, and other GTE locations are in the area. Personnel can be reached at (703) 818-4464; the fax number is (703) 818-5484.

Hadley Memorial Hospital

Personnel
4601 Martin Luther King, Jr. Avenue, SW
Washington, DC 20032
(202) 574-5726

HMH is a general hospital located in southwest Washington, DC, employing nurses, clinicians, technicians, and clerical, service, and maintenance workers. Support personnel may apply in person Mondays and Wednesdays, 1:00 p.m.-4:00 p.m. Clinicians and nurses may apply Monday-Friday, 8:30 a.m.-5:00 p.m. DC licensure is required for nurses. For more information, call Personnel at (202) 574-5725. The fax number is (202) 373-5906.

Hechinger

Human Resources Office
1616 McCormick Drive
Landover, MD 20785
(301) 341-0526

Hechinger is a do-it-yourself home improvement retail chain, employing sales, security, computer, clerical, and executive workers. Jobs are located in Maryland, Virginia, and Washington, DC. The Human Resources office is near the Landover Metro Station, and can be reached at (301) 341-1000, x3725.

Hilton

see Washington Hilton and Towers

Holiday Inn Crowne Plaza Rockville

1750 Rockville Pike
Rockville, MD 20852
(301) 468-6470

This Holiday Inn hires front desk, service, housekeeping, accounting, maintenance, sales, catering, and managerial personnel. Apply in person 8:00 a.m.-5:00 p.m. The hotel is near the Twinbrook Metro Stop. For more information, call Personnel at 468-1100.

Holy Cross Hospital

Employment Services
1500 Forest Glen Road
Silver Spring, MD 20910
(703) 538-2235 (touch-tone)
x777—patient care positions
x888—nonpatient care positions
x999—to request application

HCH is an acute-care teaching hospital located in Silver Spring, MD, visible from the Capital Beltway. They advertise these positions on the jobline: clerical, communications, social service, professional, clinical, nursing, technical, maintenance, and directors. Write down the job numbers to access more information through the touch-tone extension system. Use the job titles when applying in person or through the mail. Call the nursing recruiter at (301) 905-1027 and Employment Services at (301) 905-1374. The TDD number is (301) 905-1414.

Howard University and Hospital

Employment Services
400 Bryant Street, NW
Washington, DC 20059
(202) 806-7711/2

This is an educational institution involved in research, teaching, and medical treatment. Their jobline advertises technical, pharmacy, maintenance, administrative, managerial, accounting, clerical, service, library, clinical, nursing, computer, communications, and support positions. Faculty and physician vacancies are not on the jobline. The jobline is a tape loop, so it will replay after rewinding. Employment recommends applying in person. They can also be reached at (202) 806-7713.

Hyatt Regency Crystal City

Human Resources
2799 Jefferson Davis Highway
Arlington, VA 22202
(703) 418-7228

The Hyatt Regency is part of the national Hyatt hospitality chain. They hire administrative, financial, management, service, and maintenance personnel. Apply in person Monday and Wednesday 9:00 a.m.-noon, and Tuesday 2:30 p.m.-5:30 p.m. It is located near the Crystal City Metro Station. Call (703) 418-1234 and ask for Human Resources.

ICF International, Inc.

Human Resources
9300 Lee Highway
Fairfax, VA 22031-1207
(703) 934-3179

ICF is a leader in environment, infrastructure, energy, health care, and information technology. Its subsidiaries include ICF, Inc.; ICF Resources; ICF Information Technology; ICF Kaiser Engineers Group; Clement Associates, Inc.; and Lewin ICF. They do not advertise vacancies but screen résumés for research assistants, public policy experts, economists, engineers, scientists, computer professionals, accountants, contracts administrators, and secretaries. Jobs are located throughout northern Virginia. Send a résumé, which will be acknowledged by a postcard receipt. Résumés are kept on file for one year. The fax number is (703) 591-3699. New graduates should also include transcripts. Human Resources will contact applicants for interviews and prefers not to receive telephone inquiry.

International Business Machines Corporation

Resource and Employment Office
3-B-2
1301 K Street, NW
Washington, DC 20005-3307
(202) 515-5900
or
Employment Department
Federal Sector Division
9500 Godwin Drive
Manassas, VA 22110
(703) 367-0728
or
Personnel
2277 Research Boulevard
Fourth Floor
Rockville, MD 20850
(301) 640-5434

IBM is a top-level business and high-tech employer. They hire electronic technicians, engineers, computer programmers, marketers, and administrative staff. The Manassas facility designs and manufactures federal business systems. Call (703) 367-2804 for manufacturing job information and (703) 367-0708 for professional job information. These extensions can be requested at (800) 922-9111 during business hours. Additional facilities are located in Bethesda, Rockville, Gaithersburg, and Beltsville, MD; and Arlington, Reston, and Vienna, VA.

Jefferson Hospital

Human Resources
4600 King Street
Alexandria, VA 22302-9988
(703) 998-4965

Jefferson Hospital is a 120-bed acute-care facility. It may have openings in accounting, technical, clerical, clinical, administration, and nursing jobs. To request an application, leave your name and address after the message tone or apply in person 10:00 a.m.-3:00 p.m. Call the nursing recruiter at (703) 998-4825 and Human Resources at (703) 998-4875.

Kaiser Engineers

see ICF International, Inc.

Kaiser Permanente

Human Resources
PO Box 9733
4200 Wisconsin Avenue, NW
Washington, DC 20016
(800) 326-4005 (touch-tone
x1—nursing
x2—specialty clinical
x3—all others
x4—KP news

Kaiser Permanente, a health maintenance organization with branches in the metropolitan Washington and Baltimore areas, employs a wide variety of clinical, technical, clerical, support, professional, and maintenance positions. Physician vacancies are not included. The Human Resources office is located near the Tenleytown Metro Station and can be reached at (202) 364-3444/5. The TDD number is (202) 364-0027.

Labat-Anderson, Inc.

Staffing Specialist
2200 Clarendon Boulevard
Suite 900
Arlington, VA 22201
(703) 525-5300, x250 (touch-tone)
(703) 525-9400, ask for extension 250 (rotary)

Labat-Anderson is a high-tech services company with an administrative office near the Court House Metro Station. They may advertise computer professional, editor, librarian, technician, environmental analyst, and executive assistant positions. Jobs are located in Rockville and Suitland, MD; Rosslyn, VA; and Washington, DC, near the L'Enfant Plaza Metro Station. Some require a security clearance. Staffing prefers to receive résumés by mail or fax at (703) 525-7975; they do not accept unsolicited résumés. For more information, leave a message after the jobline. The receptionist also has job listings at the front desk.

Lewin ICF

see ICF International, Inc.

Loyola Federal Savings and Loan Association

Human Resources
1300 North Charles Street
Baltimore, MD 21201
or

Operations Center
Human Resources
1000 Stewart Avenue
Glen Burnie, MD 21061
(301) 332-2020
(301) 470-7250, x2020 (local to Washington)

This financial services institution has 37 branches in Baltimore and surrounding areas in Maryland. The operations center, close to Baltimore-Washington International Airport, has all computer jobs. The bank employs tellers, clerical and support workers, managers, and accountants. For more information about a specific vacancy, refer to the job posting in Human Resources or call the telephone number indicated on the jobline. The main Human Resources is near the State Center Metro Station.

Manor Care, Inc.

Employment Department
10770 Columbia Pike
Silver Spring, MD 20901
(800) 348-2041 (touch-tone)
x1—secretarial and clerical
x2—professionals in Manor Care Health Care Corporation
x3—professionals in Choice Hotel International
x4—professionals in Manor Care, Inc.
x5—nurse management training and administrator in training programs

Manor Care, holding company for Manor Care Healthcare residential facilities, Choice Hotels International, and Quality Inns, has its corporate offices in Silver Spring, MD. Benefits include free parking, tuition reimbursement, child care discount, employee cafeteria, and on-site health club. They hire clerical (temporary work available), clinical, management, financial, computer, maintenance, service, and nursing staff. All jobs are located at the headquarters unless otherwise noted. Employment recommends mailing your résumé only for vacant positions together with your salary requirements. For more information, call (301) 593-9600, x4469. They also accept résumés by fax at (301) 681-8740.

Marriott Hotels and Resorts

1 Marriott Drive
Bethesda, MD 20817
(703) 461-6100 (touch-tone)

x1—job opportunities
    x1—restaurant, banquet, food preparation
    x2—housekeeping, front desk, gift shop
    x3—administrative, clerical
    x4—engineering, maintenance
    x5—repeat message
(703) 461-6115 Spanish (Español)
(703) 461-6109 Gaithersburg only

Marriott operates the top lodging chain in the United States. Their joblines cover hotels in Washington, suburban Maryland, and northern Virginia. Marriott hires workers as listed above. Benefits include tuition and hotel discounts. Applications are placed at the hotel for which the opening was announced. Personnel also keeps applications on file. Addresses and directions are provided on the jobline. Many of the hotels have access to Metrorail. Refer also to each personnel department for more information.

Maryland Casualty Company

Employment Department
3910 Keswick Road
Baltimore, MD 21211
(800) 462-2562 (touch-tone)
x1—Baltimore vacancies
x2—national vacancies

The new Maryland Casualty Company is a property and casualty insurance company belonging to the Zurich group of insurers. Maryland Casualty has been operating since 1898. They employ underwriters, marketers, claims adjusters, accountants, data processors, administrative workers, and additional temporary personnel. Call Employment during business hours at (800) 462-2562 after listening to the recording. The fax number is (301) 338-9222.

Maryland Library Association

115 West Franklin Street
Baltimore, MD 21218
(301) 685-5760

MLA is Maryland's branch of the National Library Association. Their jobline lists vacancies in the library and information resource fields. MLA lists vacancies in Maryland, Virginia, Washington, DC, and nationally. Apply with individual listings, or Monday-Thursday mornings at MLA near the Lexington Market Metro Station. Call the office at (301) 727-7422, 9:30 a.m.-2:30 p.m.

Maryland Natural Gas

see Washington Gas Light Company

McDonald's

Personnel
3015 Williams Drive
Fairfax, VA 22031
(703) 698-4001 (touch-tone)
x4327—job information

McDonald's, an international fast food chain, lists recruiting information on this jobline. They hire crew members, managers, and administrators. McDonald's Corporation Training Center ("Hamburger High") is located near the corporate offices. For more information, leave your name and number at the message tone or call (703) 698-4000 and ask for Personnel.

MCI International

Human Resources
Department 0313-JL
601 South 12th Street
Arlington, VA 22202
or
Human Resources
Department 0099-JL
1650 Tyson's Boulevard
McLean, VA 22102
(703) 486-6420 (touch-tone)
x1—financial, accounting, legal, regulatory, corporate, administrative,
    human resources, support, and maintenance
x2—marketing, advertising, public relations, sales, government sales,
    clerical, communications, and clerical
(800) 289-0128, for engineering, management, and operations

MCI is an international telecommunications service company, hiring professionals as listed above. The Arlington office is located near the Pentagon City Metro Station. Applicants must submit a résumé including salary requirements and the requisition number to the address designated on the jobline. Call the Arlington office at (703) 486-3000.

Media General Cable of Fairfax

Human Resources
14650 Lee Road
Chantilly, VA 22021
(703) 378-3440

Media General Cable of Fairfax is a cable television utility company serving northern Virginia. They hire customer service representatives, technicians, installers, plant and warehouse workers, sales representatives, "top event" representatives, telemarketers, accountants, clerks, and managers. Jobs are located in Springfield and Chantilly. Applications are accepted Monday-Friday 8:30 a.m.-4:30 p.m. A driving record from the Department of Motor Vehicles is required for all field jobs. The Human Resources office prefers not to receive telephone calls.

Memorex/Telex

Human Resources
6422 East 41st Street
Tulsa, OK 74135
(918) 628-3497
(800) 331-2623 (ask for jobline)

This national computer and audiovisual equipment company has a sales office in Springfield, VA. They employ computer, engineering, marketing, and technical professionals, as well as clerical and support workers. For the central hiring office, call (800) 331-2623 and ask for Human Resources. Call the Springfield office at (703) 719-7560.

Metpath, Inc.

Human Resources
1550 East Gude Drive
Rockville, MD 20850
or
1246 East Joppa Road
Towson, MD 21204
(301) 340-9800, x116
(800) 722-7393, x116

Metpath is a medical laboratory and patient service company. They have offices in Washington, Baltimore, suburban Maryland, and northern Virginia. They hire medical technicians, microbiologists, phlebotomists, clerks, claims adjusters, nurses, administrators, and dispatchers. The labs in Rockville, MD, are near the Rockville Metro Station. Apply in person or send your résumé. For more information, call Human Resources at (301) 340-9800, x*.

Metro Network

(703) 893-8931

Metro Network is a placement agency coordinating job fairs with federal and private employers. There is no charge to the applicant. The types of jobs offered are administrative and support positions, such as secretaries, receptionists, clerks, accountants, customer service representatives, personnel specialists, and bank tellers. Jobs are located in Washington, suburban Maryland, northern Virginia, and occasionally in Baltimore. Attend the job fairs to submit résumés or SF-171s, and to obtain interviews. Do not contact Metro Network to submit job search materials.

Mobil Oil

Employment Center
PO Box 1454
3225 Gallows Road
Merrifield, VA 22116-1454
(703) 846-2777

Mobil is a national petroleum and energy development corporation with headquarters in Fairfax, VA. They offer comprehensive benefits, contributory savings, and tuition reimbursement, and on-site banking, medical center, gift shop, free parking, and cafeteria. They accept résumés for professional positions. For clerical, legal secretary, and support openings, apply in person to complete a performance evaluation. To request an application, leave your name and address after the message tone. For more information, ask for Employment at (703) 846-3000.

Montgomery College

Human Resources
900 Hungerford Drive
Suite 130
Rockville, MD 20850
(301) 279-5373 (staff)
(301) 279-5374 (faculty)

Montgomery College is a community college with a wide range of academic offerings. The college has campuses in Rockville, Germantown, and Takoma Park (near the Takoma Park Metro Station). They may have openings in computer, development, maintenance, clerical (requires testing), or various teaching and assistant positions. Write down the vacancy title and number and request an application after the message tone. For more information, call Human Resources at (301) 279-5353.

Monumental Life

Monumental General
1111 North Charles Street
Baltimore, MD 21201
(301) 385-5995

Mon Life and Mon General are fast-paced, high-volume insurance companies. They hire clerical workers, agents, managers, accountants, and other
administrative staff. Their benefits include free lunches and tuition. The
offices are located near the State Center Metro Station. When submitting a
résumé, state the office (Mon Life or Mon General) to which it should be
sent. Applications are accepted Monday-Friday, 8:30 a.m. to 5:30 p.m. For
more information, call personnel at (301) 576-4517.

Mount Vernon Hospital

Human Resources
2501 Parker's Lane
Alexandria, VA 22306
(703) 664-7258

Mount Vernon is a general hospital with special departments in rehabilitation and cancer treatment. Nursing opportunities are included on the jobline
together with other clinical, professional, child care, support, and labor
positions. Applications are accepted 10:00 a.m.-3:00 p.m. Call Human
Resources at (703) 664-7250; the fax number is (703) 664-7235.

National Association of Broadcasters

Employment Clearinghouse
1771 N Street, NW
Washington, DC 20036
(202) 429-5498 (recording active 6:00 p.m.-8:30 a.m.)

NAB is a trade association coordinating the placement of personnel in television and radio broadcasting in the categories listed below. Call the jobline
on the designated week nights.

Monday—talent
Tuesday—sales
Wednesday—production
Thursday—engineering
Friday—news reporting

Jobs are located in Washington, DC, and nationally. To apply, send your
résumé with a cover letter to individual employers listed on the jobline and
mention NAB in the letter. Also send your résumé to NAB. The office is near

Dupont Circle and Farragut North Metro Stations. The service is free to applicants. NAB also requests applicants who obtain interviews or job offers through the NAB jobline to notify NAB of their success. For more information, call NAB at (202) 429-5498 during business hours.

National Association of Home Builders

Personnel Department
15th and M Streets, NW
Washington, DC 20005
(202) 861-2160
x1—administrative and clerical
x2—all other vacancies
x3—application information
x4—information about specific vacancies

NAHB is a national trade association coordinating residential developers. Applications are taken in the personnel office on the first floor at the above address. Résumés are accepted by mail with a cover letter stating the position title and salary requirements. NAHB is near Farragut North or McPherson Square Metro Stations. For more information, call Personnel at (202) 822-0515 or (800) 368-5242, x160.

National Broadcasting Company

Employee Relations
4001 Nebraska Avenue, NW
Washington, DC 20016
(202) 885-4058

NBC is a national television and radio network and news bureau, which broadcasts locally on WRC-TV, Channel 4. Employment opportunities include computer, clerical, and marketing jobs. They also have a college intern program. The office is near the Tenleytown Metro Station. The Personnel office prefers not to receive calls and does not accept unsolicited résumés.

National Education Association

Employment Manager
Employee Relations Office
1201 16th Street, NW
Washington, DC 20036
(202) 822-7642

NEA is a trade association dealing with teaching and educational issues. They do not coordinate placement for teachers in local school districts;

however, the association employs clerical, activist, editorial, legal, support, technical, and computer professionals. Competency testing is required for some positions. Jobs are located in Washington, DC, near the Farragut North and West Metro Stations, and nationally. To apply, send your résumé with the job title and number in the cover letter. An NEA application must also be completed. NEA prefers not to receive direct telephone inquiries.

National Health Laboratories, Inc.

Personnel
13900 Park Center Road
Herndon, VA 22071
(703) 742-3193 (touch-tone)
x1—directions to office
x2—job listings

NHL is a national chain of medical testing facilities with local labs in Washington, DC, Virginia, and Maryland. They employ medical technicians, phlebotomists, drivers, aides, customer service representatives, accountants, and clerks. Applications are accepted in person or by résumé. For more information, call the phlebotomist recruiter at (703) 741-3120. For Personnel, call (800) 372-3734 from inside Virginia; (800) 336-0391 outside Virginia; or (703) 742-3100 and ask for Personnel.

National Public Radio

Personnel Department
2025 M Street, NW
Washington, DC 20036
(202) 822-2777 (touch-tone)
x1—administrative
x2—technical
x3—programming
x8—all others

x9—leave message requesting NPR application, including job number and title
x0—return to beginning of message

NPR is the national free radio service offering news, music, and educational programming. They employ technical, administrative, marketing, support, computer, clerical, production, editing, managerial, accounting, and announcing professionals. The office is near the Dupont Circle Metro Station. For more information, call Personnel at (202) 822-2909, 10:30 a.m.-2:30 p.m.

National Rehabilitation Hospital

Human Resources Services
102 Irving Street, NW
Washington, DC 20010
(202) 877-1700

NRH is a nonprofit treatment facility specializing in care for persons with serious disability. They employ a wide range of professional and clinical rehabilitation professionals, as well as support and administrative personnel. All applicants must provide proof of the right to work in the United States and must provide one or more of the following: a passport, employment authorization (green card), birth certificate, Social Security card, or driver's license. The TDD number is (202) 877-1450. Human Resources can be reached at (202) 877-1715. For recruiters, call nursing at (202) 877-1680, physical therapy at (202) 877-1510, and occupational therapy at (202) 877-1023.

National Research, Inc.

5335 Wisconsin Avenue, NW
Suite 710
Washington, DC 20015
(202) 686-9743

This is a national telephone research/survey firm. The jobline advertises telephone interviewer positions only; a clear English-speaking voice is required. The jobline may be turned off if there are no vacancies. The office is near the Friendship Heights Metro Station. To apply, call (202) 686-2406 and have that day's *Washington Post* in hand to read aloud. Calling the office directly constitutes your first interview.

Nature Conservancy, The

Human Resources
1815 North Lynn Street
Arlington, VA 22209
(703) 247-3721

The Nature Conservancy conducts environmental research and protects endangered species and natural communities. The headquarters are located in Arlington near the Rosslyn Metro Station. The jobline announces weekly positions nationwide. They hire biologists, botanists, agriculturalists, public relations, administrators, and related environmental professionals. Submit your résumé as directed. For more information, call the office with the vacancy or call (703) 841-5379.

Potomac Electric Power Company

Employment Department
1900 Pennsylvania Avenue, NW
Suite 100
Washington, DC 20068
(202) 872-2100

PEPCO is a Washington area electrical utility company employing clerical, legal, computer, engineering, supervisory, and union personnel. Jobs are located in Washington, DC, Virginia, and Maryland. Apply in person on Wednesday 10:00 a.m.-4:00 p.m. The office is near the Farragut North and West Metro Stations. Résumés are also accepted for specific job vacancies. For more information, call Employment at (202) 872-2101.

Potomac Hospital

Personnel
2300 Opitz Boulevard
Woodbridge, VA 22191
(703) 670-1836

Potomac is the largest medical facility in Prince William County. They may recruit nurses, clinicians, technicians, clerks, administrators, and housekeepers. Send a résumé or apply in person. For more information, call (703) 670-1509.

Prince George's Hospital Center

Human Resources Department
3001 Hospital Drive
Cheverly, MD 20785
(301) 618-2261

PGHC is a general hospital beside the Baltimore-Washington Parkway close to the Maryland and Washington border. They employ technical, clinical, pharmacy, nursing, clerical, communications, computer, inventory, support, professional, accounting, and child care workers. The hospital is near the Cheverly Metro Station. Apply in person. For more information, call Personnel at (301) 618-2260, x3; the nurse recruiter can be reached at x4.

Professional Resources OnLine

2011 Crystal Drive
Suite 813
Arlington, VA 22202-3721
(800) 866-1808 (touch-tone)

x1—resource management, logistical support
x2—computer
x3—engineering
x4—administration

PRO is a technical management search firm that pays you—$250-$750—to accept jobs they identify for you. They coordinate technical, engineering, scientific, administrative, and computer hiring. Request a skills profile after the message tone and return it to PRO by mail. Employers will then contact you to arrange interviews. Their computer listings are confidential, and their staff provides you the option (for a fee) of being notified before an employer will call. Your résumé will remain online until you notify PRO otherwise.

Providence Hospital

Employment Office
1150 Varnum Street, NE
Washington, DC 20017
(202) 269-7923

This is a general hospital with special departments, including the Women's Health Center and the Wellness Express. They employ clerical, clinical, technical, professional, supervisory, support, communications, security, safety, inventory, accounting, and service workers. Apply in person for specific vacancies 9:00 a.m.-noon and 1:00-3:00 p.m. at the Employment Office near the Brookland Metro Station. Nursing positions are not included on the jobline. For nursing information call (202) 269-7925. Applicants may call Employment at (202) 269-7928.

Provident Bank of Maryland

Employment
7210 Ambassador Road
Woodlawn, MD 21207
(301) 281-7263 (touch-tone)
x1—tellers
x2—all other vacancies

This Maryland financial institution employs loan counselors as well as clerical, administrative, computer, insurance, customer service, mortgage, accounting, and communications workers. To apply, list the job at the top of your résumé and include salary requirements and daytime telephone number. For more information, call Employment at (301) 281-7280.

Quest Systems, Inc.

6400 Goldsboro Road
Department AB
Bethesda, MD 20817
(301) 229-2200

This computer and communications placement agency charges no fee to applicants. The agency offers all levels of professional jobs, but applicants must have at least two years of professional computing experience to apply. Call the office to receive their free Opportunity Bulletin. For more information about Maryland, Virginia, and Washington, DC, vacancies and to register, call (301) 229-4200. The fax number is (301) 229-0965.

Radisson Plaza Hotel at Mark Center

Personnel
5000 Seminary Road
Alexandria, VA 22311
(703) 671-2483

The Radisson is a 500-room luxury hotel visible from Interstate 395. The jobline may advertise personal service, fine dining service, transportation, management, housekeeping, maintenance, clerical, and administration jobs. Apply in person or send your résumé. Personnel prefers not to receive telephone calls but will accept résumés by fax at (703) 820-6425.

Recruiting New Teachers, Inc.

385 Concord Avenue
Suite 100
Belmont, MA 02178-9804
(800) 458-3224

Recruiting New Teachers does not provide specific job leads but serves as a clearing-house of information on the teaching profession. Leave your name and address on the toll-free number, and they will send you a brochure about how to enter the teaching profession. Further information is available about teacher education/financial aid, certification, alternative certification/mid-career, and minority opportunities; other information is available on how to find a teaching job. There is also information on elementary, intermediate, secondary, special education, English as a second language, bilingual, and math/science specializations. For more information, call the National Education Association at (202) 833-4000 or the American Federation of Teachers at (202) 879-4400.

Safeway

Employment Office
5515 Kenilworth Avenue
Riverdale, MD 20737 (Maryland and District stores)
or
9639 Lost Knife Road
Gaithersburg, MD 20879 (Upper Montgomery County stores)
or
7700 Little River Turnpike
Annandale, VA 22003 (Virginia stores)
(301) 779-6101

This retail grocery chain has stores in the Washington metropolitan area. Safeway does not post job openings but collects applications to keep on file for 60 days. To apply, pick up an application at any store and mail it to the appropriate employment office. For more information, call the Riverdale office at (301) 779-6102; they are open 9:00-11:30 a.m. and 1:00-3:30 p.m. The Gaithersburg office accepts applications only by mail, and can be reached at (301) 948-2324. The Annandale office is open on Monday 11:00 a.m.-7:00 p.m.; on Tuesday and Wednesday 1:00 p.m.-9:00 p.m.; and Thursday and Friday 9:00 a.m.-5:00 p.m. They can be reached at (703) 941-0675.

7-Eleven

Southland Corporation
5300 Shawnee Road
Alexandria, VA 22312
(800) 562-0711

7-Eleven is an international convenience store chain. Applications for crew members are accepted in person at any store, while management vacancies are discussed on the jobline. For Maryland management information, call (703) 658-8581; for Virginia management information, call (703) 658-8522.

Sibley Memorial Hospital

Human Resources
5255 Loughboro Road, NW
Washington, DC 20016
(202) 364-8665

Sibley is a medical-surgical hospital located in northwest Washington, DC. The jobline may include vacancies in clerical, computer, utilization review, service, support, technical, clinical, maintenance, and others. Apply in person Monday-Thursday, 9:00 a.m.-4:00 p.m. Nurses may call (202) 537-4333. For more information, call Human Resources at (202) 537-4000.

Sprint International

Human Resources
12490 Sunrise Valley Drive
Reston, VA 22096
(703) 698-7900 (touch-tone)
x1—job listings
x2—directions
x3—résumé status

Sprint is an international long-distance telephone service utility. It may have jobs open in planning, operations, marketing, training, sales, technician, management, administration, accounting, analysis, computer, and library work. Mail your résumé or fax it to (703) 698-7263. Call Human Resources at (703) 698-7900, x0.

Suburban Hospital

Human Resources
8600 Old Georgetown Road
Bethesda, MD 20814
(301) 530-3131 (touch-tone)
x1—job listings
    x1—nursing
    x2—allied health
    x3—administrative, clerical, and support
    x4—miscellaneous
    x5—repeat sequence

Suburban is a general hospital in lower Montgomery County, MD. They have special departments in shock trauma and gerontology. The jobline may list mechanical, clinical, technical, service, professional, housekeeping, accounting, printing, clerical, and computer jobs. Call Human Resources at (301) 530-3131, x6, or (301) 530-3830. The fax number is (301) 493-5583.

"Sunline"

(301) 783-2525 (touch-tone)
x1—to leave résumé for a new ad
x2—to listen to the company's response to your résumé
x3—for companies to listen to résumé responses
x4—audio demonstration of "Sunline"
x5—to customize your résumé questions

This jobline is coordinated by the *Baltimore Sun* for applicants to check their application status on advertised job vacancies, and for employers to provide information for classified ads and check applicants who leave messages. The types of jobs and locations depend on the employers using this service.

Teleconectics Job Bank Line

PO Box 1241
Lanham Station
Seabrook, MD 20706
(301) 577-9150 (touch-tone)
x1, then x2—job listings

This is a career search firm, coordinating hiring in Maryland, Virginia, and Washington, DC. The jobline has a "voice résumé" option, which allows employers to contact applicants for further information. Also apply with the employers directly as described on the jobline. They have technical, professional, banking, construction, marketing, medical, clerical, and other occupations listed. The fax number is (301) 577-2433; for more information, call (301) 577-2373. Teleconectics does not accept résumés for employers.

Times-Journal Company, The

Human Resources
6883 Commercial Drive
Springfield, VA 22159
(703) 750-7435

This company publishes the daily and weekly county and military newspapers. Occupations are in four categories: editorial (including journalists), administrative (including computer, maintenance, clerical, and couriers), sales (including advertising and telemarketing), and production (including handlers, graphic artists, press trainees, and technicians). They also offer an intern-for-credit program. Jobs are located in Virginia and Maryland. Apply on Tuesday 9:00 a.m.-1:00 p.m. and 2:00 p.m.-4:00 p.m., or send your résumé. Telemarketers call (703) 750-7417 to apply. The TDD number is (703) 671-3323. For more information, call Human Resources at (703) 750-8133. The fax number is (703) 642-7392.

Tracor Applied Sciences, Inc.

Personnel Department
1601 Research Boulevard
Rockville, MD 20850
(301) 279-4646

Tracor is a defense contractor, providing engineering and technical support. They hire engineers, computer professionals, project managers, clerks, and administrators. Jobs are located in Rockville, Arlington, VA (near the Crystal City Metro Station), and nationally. For more information and application materials, call Personnel at (301) 279-4233 or (800) 638-8512. The clerical and administrative recruiter can be reached at (301) 279-4518.

University of Maryland at College Park

Personnel Services Department
College Park, MD 20740-3121
or
Administrative Services Building, #338
Room 1104
Paint Branch Drive
College Park, MD 20740
(301) 405-5677 (touch-tone) (also TDD accessible)
x1,

x1—directions, benefits	x8—repeat this sequence
x2—job listings	x9—main menu
x3—to request an application	x0—operator

This is the flagship campus of Maryland's state-funded higher education system, one of eleven institutions throughout the state. Classified (hourly) jobs include clerical, technical, maintenance, and security. Associate (professional) jobs include academic support, administrative, research, computer, library, accounting, planning, and development. Faculty jobs are also included. Associate and faculty applicants must send résumés directly to the department with the vacancy (call (301) 405-1000 for more information). For classified jobs, apply in person 8:30 a.m.-noon. For more information, call Employment at (301) 405-5677, x0, which is also TDD accessible.

Urban Institute

Personnel
2100 M Street, NW
Washington, DC 20037
(202) 857-8604

The Urban Institute is a nonprofit public policy research organization, specializing in domestic and international issues, such as health policy and child care. They may hire economists, public policy experts, health policy experts, demographers, research analysts, and engineers, as well as support staff. The office is near the Foggy Bottom and Farragut West Metro Stations. For more information, call (202) 833-7200. They accept résumés by fax at (202) 331-9747.

USAir, Inc.

Employee Relations
3800 North Liberty Street
Winston-Salem, NC 27105
(703) 418-7499

USAir is a commercial airline company with hubs in Charlotte, NC; Pittsburgh, PA; and at National Airport. The Arlington office is near the Crystal City Metro Station. They include hiring projections on their jobline for computer professionals, flight attendants and officers, and clerical, technical, and mechanical workers. They accept résumés at the above address. For hiring at other locations, call Pittsburgh at (412) 472-7693 or Winston-Salem at (919) 767-5341.

Virginia Library Association

669 South Washington Street
Alexandria, VA 22314
(703) 519-8027

VLA is the Virginia library employment clearinghouse; it coordinates referrals for Virginia openings only. Their services are free to applicants. Apply with the individual listings. For more information, call VLA at (703) 519-7853.

Virginia Power

Division Headquarters
Personnel Department
12316 Lee-Jackson Memorial Highway
Fairfax, VA 22033
(703) 359-3300

Virginia Power is an electrical and gas utility company, employing entry-level field, maintenance, meter-reading, customer service, technical, and support personnel. All jobs advertised are in northern Virginia. Apply in person at the Fairfax office on the first or third Wednesday 8:30 a.m.-11:00 a.m., or send a résumé. Applications are kept on file. Listen also for other district offices accepting applications in person. For more information, call Personnel at (703) 359-3037.

Washington Adventist Hospital

Personnel
7600 Carroll Avenue
Takoma Park, MD 20012
(301) 891-6096

Washington Adventist is a private general hospital. It may have openings in administration, computer, clerical, maintenance, clinical, social service, food service, security, or technical jobs. For more information, call the nursing recruiter at (301) 891-5847 and Personnel at (301) 891-5270. The fax number is (301) 891-5990.

Washington Gas Light Company

Employment Manager
1100 H Street, NW
Washington, DC 20080
(703) 750-5814

This local natural gas utility company includes DC Natural Gas, Northern Virginia Natural Gas, and Maryland Natural Gas. They employ accounting, drafting, legal, computer, engineering, clerical, and supervisory personnel. To apply, send a résumé. The Employment office is near the Metro Center and Gallery Place Metro Stations, and can be reached at (703) 750-5943.

Washington Hilton and Towers

Human Resources
1919 Connecticut Avenue, NW
Washington, DC 20009
(202) 797-5818

The Washington Hilton is a premier hospitality employer in the Kalorama section of Washington. It is between the Dupont Circle and Woodley Park/ Zoo Metro Stations. They employ housekeeping, spa, food service, clerical, maintenance, management, and personal service workers. Applications are accepted Monday—Wednesday 9:00 a.m. to noon. For more information, call Personnel at (202) 483-3000.

Washington Hospital Center

Employment Director
110 Irving Street, NW
Room 1-A-66
Washington, DC 20010-2975
(202) 877-7451

WHC is a nationally known tertiary care facility, employing clerical, clinical, technical, operational, and professional personnel. Nursing opportunities are not included on the jobline. Apply in person Monday - Friday 9:00 a.m.-4:00 p.m., or send a résumé. For more information, call Human Resources at (202) 877-6796 or (800) 232-0979.

Washington Metropolitan Area Transit Authority

Employment
600 5th Street, NW
Washington, DC 20001
(703) 538-3350 (touch-tone)
x8888—jobs open this week
x9999—application request

WMATA, or "Metro," is the office handling Metrorail and Metrobus public transportation for the Washington metropolitan area. The jobline advertises clerical, communications, administrative, planning, engineering, and driving positions. To apply, use a Metro application obtained at the office, near Gallery Place and Judicial Square Metro Stations, or at any Metro garage. The TDD number is (202) 638-3780. Call Employment at (202) 962-1071.

Washington Personnel Association

PO Box 39259
Washington, DC 20016
(202) 966-5627

This association coordinates professional (exempt) Human Resources employment opportunities in the Washington metropolitan area. There is no fee to applicants. Apply with individual jobline listings, and not with WPA. For more information, call the office at (202) 966-1258.

Washington Post

Employment Department
1150 15th Street, NW
Washington, DC 20071
(202) 334-5350

The *Washington Post* is a daily newspaper, read worldwide. They hire inserters (who must apply directly at the production plants), accounting, sales, advertising, customer service, technical, maintenance, clerical, security, and laborers. Jobs are located in Washington, DC, and Virginia. Delivery drivers can call (202) 334-6100 to apply. News applicants can send a résumé in care of the News Department. All other applicants should send a résumé in care of Employment. The Employment office is near McPherson Square Metro Station and does not accept telephone calls.

Washington Times

Human Resources
3400 New York Avenue, NE
Washington, DC 20002
(202) 636-4700 (touch-tone)

x1—job listings
x2—carrier information
x3—telemarketing information
x4—editing information

The *Washington Times* is a daily newspaper. Employment there includes carriers, clerks, support, marketing, accounting, computer, customer service, security, copy writing, and quality control. To apply, send a résumé. Human Resources prefers not to receive applications in person or by direct telephone inquiry. The fax number is (202) 526-6820.

WDCA, Channel 20

Personnel
5202 River Road
Bethesda, MD 20816
(301) 654-2600, ask for jobline
(operational during business hours only)

WDCA is an independent commercial television station. They accept résumés
for sales, administration, interns, clerks, and technical production personnel. Personnel will not accept telephone calls.

WETA, Channel 26 and FM-91

Human Resources Department
PO Box 2626
Washington, DC 20013
or
3700 South Four Mile Run Drive
Arlington, VA 22206
(703) 820-6025

WETA is a public television station whose jobline vacancies may include administrative, support, development, and accounting positions; only a limited number of jobs are available in television and radio production. Jobs are located in Shirlington, VA. For more information, call (703) 998-2759. The fax number is (703) 824-8343.

WJLA, Channel 7

Attention: (appropriate administrator)
3007 Tilden Street, NW
Washington, DC 20008
(202) 364-7914

WJLA is a commercial television station of the ABC Network, employing news, sales, production, clerical, editing, and administrative personnel. Send résumé to the administrator listed for each opening. The station is near the Cleveland Park Metro Station. Personnel prefers not to receive calls.

WTTG—Fox Channel 5

Personnel
5151 Wisconsin Avenue, NW
Washington, DC 20016
(202) 895-3233

WTTG is a commercial station on the Fox Television Network. Possible positions include producer, director, sales, engineering, accounting, clerical, and administrative. The station is near the Friendship Heights Metro Station. For more information, call Personnel at (202) 895-3232.

WUSA, Channel 9

Personnel Manager
4001 Brandywine Street, NW
Washington, DC 20016
(202) 364-3783

WUSA is a commercial television station, broadcasting on the CBS Network. They employ production, clerical, engineering, reporting/writing, and administrative personnel. "Talent," or announcing, positions are not included on the jobline. The station is near the Tenleytown Metro Station. For more information, call Personnel at (202) 364-3780.

Appendix D

EMPLOYER CONTACT FORM

Employer: _____

Address: _____ Phone: (____) _____

_____ Contact: _____

Openings: (note location, vacancy announcement numbers, salaries, closing dates, etc.)

_____

_____

Application recommendations: _____

Date Applied: _____

Interview: _____

Follow-up: _____

Notes: _____

_____

Appendix E
VITA **WORK SHEET**

Whole Name: _____

Maiden or alias: _____

Birth date: _____ Social Security Number: _____

Driver's License Number: _____ Expiration/Points: _____

Hobbies: _____

Interests: _____

Magazine Subscriptions: _____

High School/GED: _____

    Dates attended: ___/___ to ___/___ Location: _____

    Studies: _____ GPA: _____

College: _____

    Dates attended: ___/___ to ___/___ Location: _____

    Major: _____ GPA: _____

    Internships: _____

    Research Projects: _____

    Awards/Honors: _____

    Publications: _____

    Memberships: _____

(repeat as needed)

Additional Classes: _____

    School: _____ Dates: _____ Location: _____

Union Membership: _____ Local #: _____

    Dates: _____/_____to_____/_____ Certification: _____

    Location: _____ Phone:(_____) _____

Military Branch: _____ Training: _____

    Dates: _____ Location:_____

    Discharge Type _____ Awards: _____

Employer: _____ Job Title: _____

Location: _____ Dates: _____/_____to_____/_____

Salary: _____ Supervisor: _____

Telephone: (_____) _____ Reason for Leaving: _____

Promotions: _____

Job Tasks (% of time spent):

Supervising Duties:

Machines Operated:

Computer Skills:

(repeat as needed)

Additional Skills: _____

Foreign Languages: _____

Publications: _____

Memberships: _____

Certifications: _____

Licensures: _____

Glossary

Administrative Careers with America—a federal program coordinating entry-level jobs for college graduates or those passing a written exam.

blue collar—refers to jobs that pay hourly wages, involve physical labor, or are classified as a trade.

career—with the federal government, a competitive position is one in the civilian executive branch; the hiring process must follow the Office of Personnel Management's regulations.

career-conditional—with the federal government, it is a job by an appointment or on a probationary period, which may last up to one year.

career path—an expected advancement progression for any given career; can be altered with additional education or experience.

closing date—the deadline for filing a job application.

cover letter—a formal business letter accompanying a résumé.

downsize—when a company decides to implement an involuntary reduction in force.

excepted—with the federal government, jobs that are excused from OPM's hiring regulations; applications are filed directly with the agency.

FFRDC—a federally funded research and development center.

follow-up—letters, telephone calls, or visits reminding the employer of the applicant's interest in the job and checking the hiring decision progress.

FTS—Federal Telephone System, the federal government's system of calling locally throughout the country.

GED—general equivalency diploma.

golden handcuffs—having a salary too high to relinquish.

GPA—grade point average.

GS pay scale—General Schedule pay scale, the federal government's pay rate divided into 18 levels with graduated increases over time. For current scales, contact any federal personnel office.

headhunter—a recruiter of personnel, especially at the corporate level.

job fair—a planned convention of employers recruiting employees, using booths or tables to conduct interviews on the spot.

jobline—an employer's telephone number, which has a recording of job openings.

job-specific résumé—a résumé designed to address specific job requirements.

KASOCs—the federal government's performance appraisal form.

networking—using personal and professional contacts to look for work.

One More Step—a method of job searching requiring persistence to enact sequential steps until receiving polite dismissal from an employer, instead of enacting one step at a time.

OPM—Office of Personnel Management, the federal government's personnel office.

performance appraisal—a sample of work performed before or during employment.

perq—or perquisite; a benefit or profit other than regular salary or wages that may or may not be taxable.

preference—procedures to give a slight advantage to applicants of specific residence, employment, minority, veteran, handicap, or other status.

references sheet—one page listing personal and/or professional references, matching the style of the résumé.

résumé—a one- or two-page document summarizing qualifications for the job target.

SF-50—Standard Form-50, the notification of personnel action confirming federal employment status; required when transferring within the federal government.

SF-171—Standard Form-171, the federal government's standard job application form used for nearly all federal vacancies; it can be obtained at any federal personnel office.

TDD—telecommunications device for the deaf.

temporary—with the federal government, it means jobs classified as not permanent, nor having official government employment status; often includes the trades and part-time work.

vacancy announcement—with the federal government, denotes a job description.

vita—a comprehensive annotation of accomplishments, experience, and education.

x—beside a number, denotes telephone extension number.

Index

The following is a comprehensive list of the employers in Appendices B and C, and the pages on which they are found, respectively.

ACTION—The National Volunteer Agency, 89
Agricultural Research Service, 90
Agriculture, US Department of, 90
Air Force District of Washington, 90
Alcohol, Drug Abuse, and Mental Health Administration, 91
Alcohol, Tobacco, and Firearms, Bureau of, 91
Alexandria, City of, 92
Alexandria City Public Schools, 92
Ameribanc Savings Bank, 132
American Medical Laboratories, Inc., 132
American Society for Training and Development, 133
American Telephone and Telegraph, 133
American University, 133
Amtrak Corporate Office, 134
Andrews Air Force Base, 92
Arbitron Ratings, 134
Arlington County, 93
Arlington County Public Schools, 93
Arms Control and Disarmament Agency, 93
Army, Department of, 94
Atlantic Research Corporation, 135
Blue Cross/Blue Shield of the National Capital Area, 135
Bridgestone/Firestone, 135
Cable News Network, 136
Cable TV Montgomery, 136
CapitalCare, 136
Catholic University of America, 137
Census, Bureau of the, 94
Center for Naval Analyses, 137
Central Intelligence Agency, 94
Chesapeake and Potomac Telephone, 137

Children's Hospital National Medical Center, 138
Commerce, US Department of, 95
Commodity Futures Trading Commission, 95
Consolidated Civilian Personnel Office, 96
Courts, US, 96
Customs Service, 96
Defense Information Systems Agency, 97
Defense Intelligence Agency, 97
Defense Logistics Agency, 98
Discovery Channel, 138
District of Columbia Government, 98
District of Columbia Public Schools, 99
District Photo, Inc., 139
Doctors' Community Hospital, 139
Eastman Kodak, 139
Education, US Department of, 99
Energy, US Department of, 100
Environmental Protection Agency, 100
Executive Office of the President, 100
Export-Import Bank of the US, 101
Fairfax, City of, 101
Fairfax, County of, 101
Fairfax County Public Schools, 102
Fairfax Hospital, 140
Fairfax Nursing Center, 140
Falls Church, City of, 102
Federal Aviation Administration, 102
Federal Deposit Insurance Corporation, 103
Federal Energy Regulatory Commission, 104
Federal Home Loan Bank Board, 104

Federal Home Loan Mortgage
  Corporation, 140
Federal Job Information Center, 104
Federal National Mortgage
  Association, 141
Federal Reserve Board, 105
First Advantage Mortgage
  Corporation, 141
First American Bank, 141
First American Reston Operations
  Center, 142
First American Staff Temporaries,
  Inc., 143
Fish and Wildlife Service, 105
Food and Drug Administration, 106
Fort Meade, 106
Fort Ritchie, 107
Future Aviation Professionals of
  America, 143
Gallaudet University, 144
Gannett Company, Inc., 144
General Accounting Office, 107
Geological Survey, US, 108
George Mason University, 108
Georgetown University, 144
Georgetown University Hospital, 145
Giant Food, 145
Goddard Space Flight Center, 108
Greater Laurel-Beltsville
  Hospital, 146
Greater Southeast Community
  Hospital, 146
Group Health Association, 147
GTE Government Systems, 147
Hadley Memorial Hospital, 147
Health Resources and Services
  Administration, 109
Hechinger, 148
Holiday Inn Crowne Plaza
  Rockville, 148
Holy Cross Hospital, 148
House Placement Office, 109
Housing and Urban
  Development, 110
Howard County, 110
Howard County Schools, 110
Howard University and
  Hospital, 149
Hyatt Regency Crystal City, 149
ICF International, Inc., 149
Immigration and Naturalization
  Service, 111

Indian Affairs, Bureau of, 111
Information Agency, US, 111
Internal Revenue Service, 112
International Business Machines
  Corporation, 150
Jefferson Hospital, 150
Justice, US Department of, 112
Kaiser Permanente, 151
Labat-Anderson, Inc., 151
Labor, Department of, 112
Library of Congress, 113
Loudoun, County of, 113
Loyola Federal Savings and Loan
  Association, 151
Manor Care, Inc., 152
Marine Corps Headquarters, 114
Marriott Hotels and Resorts, 152
Maryland Casualty Company, 153
Maryland Library Association, 153
Maryland-National Capital Park and
  Planning Commission, 114
Maryland State Government, 115
McDonald's, 154
MCI International, 154
Media General Cable of Fairfax, 154
Memorex/Telex, 155
Merit Systems Protection
  Board, 115
Metpath, Inc., 155
Metro Network, 156
Minerals Management Service, 116
Mines, Bureau of, 116
Mobil Oil, 156
Montgomery College, 156
Montgomery County, 116
Montgomery County Public
  Schools, 117
Monumental Life, 157
Mount Vernon Hospital, 157
National Aeronautics and Space
  Administration, 117
National Association of
  Broadcasters, 157
National Association of Home
  Builders, 158
National Association of Securities
  Dealers, 117
National Broadcasting
  Company, 158
National Cancer Institute, 118
National Education Association, 158
National Gallery of Art, 118

National Health Laboratories,
Inc., 159
National Institute of Standards and
Technology, 119
National Institutes of Health, 119
National Park Service, 120
National Public Radio, 159
National Rehabilitation
Hospital, 160
National Research, Inc., 160
National Security Agency, 120
National Technical Information
Service, 120
Nature Conservancy, The, 160
Naval Academy, US, 121
Naval Air Station, Patuxent
River, 121
Northern Virginia Community
College, 121
Northern Virginia Training
Center, 122
Overseas Private Investment
Corporation, 122
Patent and Trademark Office, 122
Peace Corps, 123
Postal Service, US, 123
Potomac Electric Power
Company, 161
Potomac Hospital, 161
Prince George's County, 124
Prince George's County Public
Schools, 124
Prince George's Hospital Center, 161
Prince William County, 124
Prince William County Public
Schools, 125
Professional Resources OnLine, 161
Providence Hospital, 162
Provident Bank of Maryland, 162
Public Debt, Bureau of the, 125
Public Health Service, 125
Quest Systems, Inc., 163
Radisson Plaza Hotel at Mark
Center, 163
Recruiting New Teachers, Inc., 163

Safeway, 164
Senate Placement Office, 126
7-Eleven, 164
Sibley Memorial Hospital, 164
Small Business Administration, 126
Smithsonian Institution, The, 127
Sprint International, 165
State, Department of, 128
Suburban Hospital, 165
"Sunline", 165
Supreme Court of the US, 128
Teleconectics Job Bank Line, 166
Times-Journal Company, The, 166
Tracor Applied Sciences, Inc., 166
Transportation, US Department
of, 128
Treasury, US Department of, 129
University of Maryland at College
Park, 167
Urban Institute, 167
USAir, Inc., 168
Veterans' Administration Medical
Center, 129
Virginia, Commonwealth of, 130
Virginia Library Association, 168
Virginia Power, 168
Voice of America, 130
Washington Adventist Hospital, 168
Washington Convention Center, 130
Washington Gas Light
Company, 169
Washington Hilton and Towers, 169
Washington Hospital Center, 169
Washington Metropolitan Area
Transit Authority, 170
Washington Navy Yard, 131
Washington Personnel
Association, 170
Washington Post, 170
Washington Times, 170
WDCA, Channel 20, 171
WETA, Channel 26 and FM-91, 171
WJLA, Channel 7, 171
WTTG—Fox Channel 5, 172
WUSA, Channel 9, 172